THE
VERY BEST,
HANDS-ON,
KINDA DANGEROUS
FAMILY
DEVOTIONS

Volume 2

THE VERY BEST, HANDS-ON, KINDA DANGEROUS FAMILY DEVOTIONS

52 ACTIVITIES YOUR KIDS WILL NEVER FORGET

Volume 2

TIM SHOEMAKER

Revell

a division of Baker Publishing Group
Grand Rapids, Michigan

© 2023 by Tim Shoemaker

Published by Revell
a division of Baker Publishing Group
Grand Rapids, Michigan
www.revellbooks.com

Printed in the United States of America

Library of Congress Cataloging-in-Publication Data
Names: Shoemaker, Tim, author.
Title: The very best, hands-on, kinda dangerous family devotions : 52 activities your kids will never forget / Tim Shoemaker.
Description: Grand Rapids : Baker Publishing Group, 2019.
Identifiers: LCCN 2018045152 | ISBN 9780800742126 (pbk.)
Subjects: LCSH: Christian education—Home training. | Christian education of children. | Object-teaching. | Families—Religious life.
Classification: LCC BV1590 .S56 2019 | DDC 249—dc23
LC record available at https://lccn.loc.gov/2018045152

All activities and projects in this book are intended to be performed under adult supervision. Appropriate and reasonable caution is required at all times, and the suggested activities cannot replace common sense and sound judgment. Observe safety and caution at all times. The author and publisher disclaim all liability for any damage, mishap, or injury that may occur from engaging in the activities featured in this book.

Published in association with Cyle Young of C.Y.L.E. (Cyle Young Literary Elite, LLC), a literary agency.

Baker Publishing Group publications use paper produced from sustainable forestry practices and post-consumer waste whenever possible.

23   24   25   26   27   28   29   7   6   5   4   3   2   1

Do not forsake me, my God,
till I declare your power to the next generation,
your mighty acts to all who are to come.
Psalm 71:18

To every mom, dad,
grandma, grandpa,
aunt, or uncle
who feels a stirring deep in their soul
as they read those words from Psalm 71.
This book is for you—
and for those kids in the next generation
who have found so much more
than a soft spot in your heart.
They own real estate there.
A room that is all theirs . . .
and always will be.

The decrees of the Lᴏʀᴅ are firm,
    and all of them are righteous.
They are more precious than gold,
    than much pure gold;
they are sweeter than honey,
    than honey from the honeycomb.
By them your servant is warned;
    in keeping them there is great reward.

                                    Psalm 19:9–11

CONTENTS

Don't have all the supplies for one of the devotionals? Borrowing is a great option . . . if you remember these three things.

—————— OBJECT LESSONS AND ACTIVITIES ——————

1. Money to Burn 29

THEME: We can trust God when we're in a tough spot.

Lighting a $20 bill on fire—and observing that it is not harmed by the fire—is something you absolutely have to see to believe. It ignites a great discussion of how we can trust God when the heat is on.

2. Gone Forever 34

THEME: God forgives our sins . . . and we should do that for others.

Throwing rocks into a lake or the ocean, never to be seen again, will remind our kids how God deals with our sin when we ask his forgiveness . . . and how we should do the same for others.

3. Minute to Win It 38

THEME: Some elements of the Christian life (like trusting and obeying God) require practice if we want to be effective.

We'll run through some classic Minute to Win It challenges to drive home the point that we only become effective with some elements of the Christian life with practice.

4. Lose the Diaper 43

THEME: Holding on to a grudge has some very unpleasant side effects.

A little experiment with a disposable diaper will help us see the importance of shedding nasty things, like resentment and grudges, instead of wearing them around like a dirty diaper.

5. Fuel on the Fire 49 ⚠

THEME: Do we add fuel to the fires of family tension—or do we calm things down?

Have you ever tossed a handful of Coffee-Mate nondairy creamer on a fire? It flares up nicely, like you've got some magic dust or powder in your hands! This will open a talk about how we have the power in our hands to make the tension or fire between us and other family members flare up—or die down. We'll have an emphasis on talking kindly to one another.

6. Bridge Builders 54

THEME: Building bridges to those who are distant from us—or isolated from others—and seeing the "unseen" and reaching out to them.

You'll need chairs for this one, or anything else you can use to build a makeshift bridge. You'll put one or two kids out on an "island" and build a bridge to get to them. This will pave the way to talk about seeing the lonely, isolated, or "unseen" kids . . . and how we can build bridges to reach them.

In this world of moving stairways and doors that open automatically, it gets pretty easy to let others do the work for us. That definitely won't work for the Christian life! Climbing up the down escalator will be a great way to demonstrate that we need to put in some effort as Christians. If we aren't constantly climbing, the world will pull us down.

A simple kids' game of Simon Says will impress on the kids that a strong start isn't enough. God is often more interested in how we finish.

A classic clown inflatable bop bag isn't only fun to hit but teaches the importance of persevering with a good attitude and a smile on our face when facing unkind words or actions, even in our own family.

A 5-gallon bucket and some fresh cement will demonstrate a simple truth: the longer we wait to step away from sin, the harder it is to break free.

The kids will run a little race—while texting on their phone the entire time. They'll be focused on the screen, and they'll overlook some important things you've planted on the route for them. This will open a talk about what we miss right around us while we're on our phones.

12. Strength Sappers 82

> THEME: Exposure to fear, worry, and anxiety can leave us weak and unprotected.

Soaking an egg in vinegar will slowly eat away at the shell, leaving an unprotected, gelatinous egg. What a great way to illustrate how exposure to fear, worry, anxiety, and more can leave us unprotected and weak!

13. Take Me to Your Leader 87

> THEME: Choosing wisely who we follow and who we shouldn't. Great leaders know who to follow . . . and who to avoid.

A little game of following another car leads to a great discussion about who our kids follow and who to avoid. Often, we want our kids to be leaders, but God wired us to be followers too. Sometimes the *best* leaders have simply learned *who* to follow.

14. Holy Howling Hex Nut 92

> THEME: The importance of listening to that voice inside us—even when we don't understand it or it scares us.

A balloon and a hex nut are all you need to talk about the importance of listening to that voice inside us—even when we don't fully understand it.

15. Hard Work Pays Off 98

> THEME: Being a good worker instead of being lazy. A good work ethic will be rewarded.

Making ice cream is hard work, but there are some nice perks. That leads right into a talk about how the Bible stresses the importance of being good workers instead of being lazy. A person who possesses a good work ethic will often be appreciated—and rewarded.

Note: The following two devotions use the same object lesson.

The Very Best HOLIDAY Devotions

A Quick Key for Parents

 Activities with this symbol are a little more on the dangerous side and will require some extra caution on your part. Additional safety tips and reminders are also included in these lessons.

INTRODUCTION

Why This Is So Important

Don't pet rattlesnakes.

Don't drive a car while blindfolded.

Don't walk down a dark alley with a wad of cash in your hand.

Don't chum the water with dead chickens before taking an ocean swim.

These are ridiculous examples of things we'd never do—because we know better. Any one of those could end with a deadly outcome. But here's a couple more examples that are even more dangerous because they have eternal consequences.

Don't leave all the spiritual training of your kids to the church.

Don't let learning about God be something that bores your kids.

You probably have a pretty good idea that the Bible tells us, especially in the book of Deuteronomy, to teach the next generation about God and the principles he's given us to live by. But why don't we do that? One big reason is that we truly don't understand the reasons for the command.

Take a look at these verses from Psalm 78, where we get the "why" behind teaching our kids about God.

> We will not hide them from their descendants;
>   we will tell the next generation
> the praiseworthy deeds of the LORD,
>   his power, and the wonders he has done.
> He decreed statutes for Jacob
>   and established the law in Israel,
> which he commanded our ancestors
>   to teach their children,
> so the next generation would know them,
>   even the children yet to be born,
>   and they in turn would tell their children.
> Then they would put their trust in God
>   and would not forget his deeds
>   but would keep his commands.
> They would not be like their ancestors—
>   a stubborn and rebellious generation,
> whose hearts were not loyal to God,
>   whose spirits were not faithful to him. (Ps. 78:4–8)

This passage gives a nod to the Deuteronomy passages ("he commanded our ancestors to teach their children") and then goes on to explain the reasons it's so critically important to teach our kids about God at home. Check out the four positive payoffs.

1. **So our kids will know God's commands—the difference between right and wrong.** See that in verse 6? "So the next generation would know them, even the children yet to be born, and they in turn would tell their children." If we don't teach

our kids, they won't know. They'll make mistakes. Get hurt. And a scary thought? The truth can be lost in one generation if parents fail to teach their kids.

2. **So our kids will trust God for salvation, of course. But also so that they'd learn to trust him and his ways, knowing God's ways are the best ways.** There it is, right in verse 7: "Then they would put their trust in God."

3. **So our kids will obey God.** Verse 7 again: "Then they would . . . keep his commands."

4. **So our kids will not forget God.** Verse 7 addresses this as well. "Then they would . . . not forget his deeds."

These four payoffs are huge. Massive. And they are all about protecting our kids, aren't they? That, my friends, is a huge motivator to lead family devotions.

As a parent, you're wired to protect. You'd jump in front of a car to save one of your kids, right? Of course you would. You'd die for them. But how far will you go to *live* for them? Will you take a chance with family devotions and change your habits a bit to carve out time for this? So your children will know God's truth. So they'll trust God. So they'll obey God. So they don't forget him. Failure always follows forgetting God . . . and none of us want this for our kids.

Family devotions are all about protecting our kids. We safeguard our kids from the lies of this world by giving them regular doses of truth—in the most appetizing way possible. So give this a try, will you? Protect your kids by teaching them about God, and do it in creative ways where they'll really listen. The church can help, but let's face it: your kids only spend an hour or so there a week. It just isn't enough. They need you to help them. To show them the way. You're the one who is there for your kids at all hours of the day or night, not the church. You can do this . . . and I want to help.

LET'S MAKE THIS EASY

You don't have to follow any order in this book. Pick devotionals that are right where your kids are at . . . or need to be. Whenever you do a devotional, jot the date in the margin next to the title in the table of contents. That way you won't repeat one unintentionally.

If you're having fun, the kids will too. Make devotional time with the family a positive experience. Yes, learning about God is serious, but you want your kids to grow up feeling that learning about God can be fun too. These devotionals aren't intended to be the type where everyone sits around the kitchen table without saying a word. Grab a snack for the kids and encourage interaction. And if they're getting loud or laughing, don't worry about quieting them down. They're still going to catch the point of the lesson, and the experience will be better for everyone!

Tim

BORROWING SUPPLIES IS A GOOD THING—IF YOU DO IT RIGHT

There will be times you'll read the list of supplies needed for a lesson and find you're short one or two essential items. Often, you'll find you can buy what you need easily and pretty cheaply. But other times you may want to borrow from family, neighbors, or friends.

There are some subtle and important advantages to borrowing that go way beyond saving money. First, borrowing opens a door of opportunity to give a word of witness to a neighbor or coworker. Or it can be a bit of encouragement to a Christian who may need to start teaching their own kids important nuggets of truth from God's Word. Second, you'll be explaining why you need the item. You may even invite the lender to join you for the little devotional time with your family so they can handle the tool or whatever it is instead of you. You'll appreciate the help, They'll appreciate feeling needed. And who knows what might happen from there.

There are three simple rules you must follow when borrowing—and they're important. These are cast in concrete, my friend. Get these three simple things right, and you'll earn respect. Miss on any one of them, and you won't be borrowing from that person again anytime soon.

1. **Return the item—*fast*.** Not when you see them next. Not when it's convenient for you. Make the effort and get whatever you borrowed back to them pronto, even if they insist there is no rush to return it. And bring the item to them. Don't ask them to come to your place.

2. **Return the item in *better condition* than you got it.** Wipe the item down. Clean it up. Coil the cord up neat and use a Velcro tie to keep it that way. If you borrow a tool with a power pack, return it fully charged. Is it gas powered? Return it with the tank full—even if you didn't use much or it was nearly empty when they loaned it to you. This is about showing you value their stuff and the chance to borrow it.

3. **Return the item with *gratitude*.** A friend who has just the thing you need at just the time you need it is a bit of a hero, don't you think? Treat them like one. Give them a big thanks. Show them a picture of you using it with the kids. Tell them how great it worked—which makes them feel smart for having it in the first place. Bring them coffee or a donut, or maybe return the tool with a bow around it, for Pete's sake. You're creative, or you never would have bought this book. Use a bit of that creativity to make the lender feel really good that they helped you out.

The three rules are easy, right? You can do this. And you'll be creating a good reputation for yourself—and being a good witness as you do.

Money to Burn

THEME: We can trust God when we're in a tough spot and the heat is on.

⚠ THINGS YOU'LL NEED

- ☐ *Isopropyl rubbing alcohol* (70%), available at any pharmacy
- ☐ *Empty glass*
- ☐ *Measuring cup* (in ounces)
- ☐ *Salt, ½ teaspoon*
- ☐ *Pair of tongs*
- ☐ *Lighter* (a stick lighter is best)
- ☐ *Safety glasses*, one pair for each of the kids—and for you too
- ☐ *$1 and $20 bill*
- ☐ *Bucket of water* (just in case)

Advance Prep

You're going to be working with fire on this one, so keep that in mind when you're choosing a spot to do this. I'd suggest doing this outside the first time. You'll also want to have a bucket filled with water nearby, just for an added measure of safety. Over the kitchen sink or bathtub works well too. Just stay clear of curtains, okay?

1. Put on your safety glasses.
2. Use the measuring cup to measure out 3 ounces of rubbing alcohol. Pour it into the glass. Put the cap on the bottle of rubbing alcohol and move it out of your way.
3. Next, measure out 1 ounce of water. Pour it into the same glass with the rubbing alcohol.
4. Add ½ teaspoon salt to the glass. Mix well with the rubbing alcohol and water.
5. Now use the tongs to stuff the $1 bill into the alcohol solution. Be sure the bill gets completely soaked. I'm suggesting you use the $1 bill here to build your confidence a bit. When you do this with the kids, the $20 bill will be much more impressive.
6. Once you're certain the entire bill has been soaked, use the tongs to remove the bill from the glass. Lift it by one corner, if possible. By doing it this way, the bill will be in a perfect position to light. Wipe up any drips of the alcohol solution that may have pooled below the bill.
7. Move the glass with the rubbing alcohol solution far from where you will be lighting the dollar bill. Have that bucket of water handy if you're not doing this over the sink or tub, just in case something doesn't go exactly right.
8. Hold the top edge of the bill by the tongs—and at a slight angle away from you if possible. Fire travels up, so you don't want

your hand in the path of the flame. Light the bottom corner of the bill with the stick lighter.

9. The bill should become enveloped in flame but remain undamaged itself. The flames should go out by themselves, leaving a perfect bill behind.

Isn't this a great experiment? Now you're ready to do it with the kids . . . but with a $20 bill this time!

Running the Activity

I'd have the alcohol solution already in the glass. Gather the kids up, have them put on their safety glasses, and get started. If your kids have their own stash of money, consider asking them to give you a $10 or $20 bill. That may increase their interest in the experiment just a little bit.

Go through the procedure as you practiced it, having the kids do as many of the steps as you feel they safely can based on their ages and level of responsibility. The more they do, the more deeply the lesson gets etched in their heads.

Once the flames have engulfed the bill and then been extinguished, you're ready to move on.

Teaching the Lesson

Something valuable, namely the $20 bill, was at stake here. If one little thing didn't go perfectly, that money would have been gone. And sometimes we face situations like that in life. We may feel something bad is going to happen unless everything goes just right.

In Daniel 3 we have the story of Daniel's three friends, Shadrach, Meshach, and Abednego, who refused to bow down to the pagan king's image. The penalty was death—by means of a very nasty fiery furnace.

Something valuable was definitely at stake here: namely, their lives. The king gave them one more chance to bow down. Listen to their answer here. The level of trust Daniel's friends had in God was fantastic.

> If we are thrown into the blazing furnace, the God we serve is able to deliver us from it, and he will deliver us from Your Majesty's hand. But even if he does not, we want you to know, Your Majesty, that we will not serve your gods or worship the image of gold you have set up. (Dan. 3:17–18)

These men trusted God. They knew he was capable of rescuing them. But even if his plan meant they were to die, they committed themselves to remain loyal to God.

When the heat is on and we are in trouble, under pressure, or facing hardship or nasty people, or when we face a culture that is increasingly hostile to genuine Christians, that is when we often find out just how real our faith in God is.

Do we really trust him?

Will we follow him, even if he doesn't answer our prayers the way we hope?

Hard times often reveal where our faith is at. And if we see our faith isn't all that it should be, we can ask God to help us with that.

Summing It Up

When we dipped the bill in rubbing alcohol and took out the lighter, it definitely must have looked like that money was going to go up in smoke. But you trusted that I'd get that money back to you, or pay you back another way, right?

Sometimes things look dark. Bleak. Like we're in a tunnel and there is no light at the end of it. Let's trust God, even though we don't see a solution. God often works in unexpected, unpredictable ways. Like the flaming $20 bill that was unharmed in the fire, or like Daniel's three friends, we can be rescued by God. But even if he lets the hard times continue for us, we must hang on all the tighter to him.

> My soul clings to you;
> your right hand upholds me. (Ps. 63:8 ESV)

This is true in both the good times and the hard. When we are facing fires, this verse reminds us of the need to cling tight to God, knowing he is holding us the whole time.

Remember, God has a way of doing the unexpected, at just the right time.

> You, LORD, keep my lamp burning;
> my God turns my darkness into light. (Ps. 18:28)

Gone Forever

THEME: **When we ask God to forgive our sins, they are gone forever . . . never to be resurrected. That should make us grateful enough to do that for others.**

THINGS YOU'LL NEED

☐ *Smooth-surfaced rocks.* They should be about the size of the palm of your hand so you have enough room to write on them but not so large that they're hard to throw. Likely you can find rocks like this outside somewhere, perhaps on the shore of whatever body of water you choose to do this. You can also check with a pet store. Often, they have bags of smooth river rock meant for aquariums that work perfectly for this.

☐ *Permanent marker* (to write on the rocks)

Advance Prep

Find a good spot on the shore of a lake, river, pond, or ocean. A pier works terrific too. And be sure you have plenty of rocks for the kids to write on and throw. The rocks will need to be clean and dry before you can write on them.

Running the Activity

1. Ask the kids to think about their sins . . . things they've done wrong but maybe haven't confessed yet. Or it could be something they did long ago, and they may have confessed it, but they still feel bad whenever it comes to mind.

2. Now have them use the marker to write that sin on a rock. Once that is done, ask them to throw it into the water, as far from shore as they can. You may want to demonstrate the first one. If the stones are flat, you may even skip some of them across the water.

3. Have them repeat this procedure as many times as they want.

4. Once they've hit a lull and seem to be out of ideas, you may want to take this a bit further. Now ask them to write ways that others have sinned against them. It could be friends, family, or really anybody. Ask if they're willing to forgive those who did them wrong. If they are ready to forgive, have them throw those rocks out into the water too.

Don't take too long on this before moving into the teaching time.

Teaching the Lesson

In Micah, a book in the Old Testament, there is a verse describing how God will forgive the sins of the nation of Israel. It gives us a great bit of insight into God's nature when it comes to how he forgives.

> You will again have compassion on us;
>> you will tread our sins underfoot
>> and hurl all our iniquities into the depths of the sea.
> (Mic. 7:19)

That word picture of hurling iniquities, or sins, into the depths of the sea is important. Think about how deep the ocean is, and picture God throwing our sins there.

- So deep, they will never surface again.
- So deep, nobody will ever find them.

That is the magnificent forgiveness he offers us when we confess our sins to him. The sins are gone. He won't dig them up again and shove them in our faces. When God forgives, it is complete. Sure, there are still consequences for our sin. If we rob a store we may go to jail—even though God forgives if we ask—right? But when God forgives, he definitely takes away the eternal punishment we deserve for that sin. That's huge! We need to let the reality of that sink in a bit. That truth should prompt some very important reactions in us.

- We should be filled with joy that our sins are forgiven, and we should love God more.
- We should be grateful that he has forgiven us so completely and desires we live in obedience to him.
- Out of that gratitude for what God did for us, we should be more willing to forgive others in the same way God forgives us.

Summing It Up

> For as high as the heavens are above the earth,
>> so great is his love for those who fear him;
> as far as the east is from the west,
>> so far has he removed our transgressions from us.
>>> (Ps. 103:11–12)

When we ask God to forgive our sins, he removes them from us completely—as far as the east is from the west. He hurls them into the deep water, never to be seen again, like those rocks we just threw. Let's be sure we're living in gratitude for God's great gift of forgiveness . . . and forgiving others the same way.

If the kids weren't ready to forgive someone who had wronged them earlier, check back to see if anybody is ready to throw another rock into the water now.

Minute to Win It

THEME: We only become effective with some elements of the Christian life (like trusting and obeying God) with practice.

THINGS YOU'LL NEED

Pretzel diving game

- ☐ *Bowl of mini pretzel twists or rings*
- ☐ *Set of chopsticks*
- ☐ *Timer*

Dizzy mummy game

- ☐ *Roll of toilet paper* for each of the kids
- ☐ *Bike helmet*
- ☐ *Timer*

Cup hands game

- [ ] *Pair of plastic 16-ounce "Solo" style cups for each of the kids*
- [ ] *Dice*, ten pair
- [ ] *Timer*

Advance Prep

Pick up supplies for one of the games above, or all three if you'd like. The games are quick, and if you can do more than one, it may help drive home the theme of the lesson just a little bit better.

Running the Activity

Choose one or more of the games above and play them with your kids. Here's how each one works.

Pretzel diving: With a chopstick between their teeth and their hands behind their back, each contestant has one minute to spear and line up as many of the mini pretzel twists from the bowl as they can on their chopstick. The one with the most pretzels on their chopstick wins!

Dizzy mummy: Each contestant clips on the bike helmet and holds the loose end of a roll of toilet paper while you spindle the roll on your fingers. Then they spin around as fast as they can until they've emptied the roll completely. The mummy who uses up the entire roll in the shortest amount of time wins! Do be careful that they don't get so dizzy they fall and get hurt, okay?

Cup hands: If you can have two of the kids go at the same time, that can be more fun. If not, just do this for time. Each contestant must wear a pair of cups on their hands and use these "cup hands" to stack dice on top of each other. The one with the tallest dice tower when the one-minute timer rings wins.

Teaching the Lesson

You've run the games and congratulated the winners. They may want to play again or get another chance to better their score. That's a great idea—but wait for all encore performances until after you've taught the lesson. If you don't, the kids could lose interest in the activity, and it will be that much harder to get them involved in the teaching time. Assure them they can have another try once you're done talking about things.

Let's start with two questions.

How many of you have ever done one of these activities before?
If I gave you time to practice, do you think you could have done better?

Yes, practice likely would have made a big difference. That's the way it is with just about anything in life. Practice will help you get better and better at whatever it is you're doing. It's that way with playing an instrument, playing sports, and just about any skill or craft you can imagine. Practice is important.

And the same is true about our Christianity. There are certain things that come easier with practice.

Do you think your faith would be stronger—and there when you need it—if you practiced trusting God more often with the little things?

Trust in the LORD with all your heart
and lean not on your own understanding;

in all your ways submit to him,
    and he will make your paths straight. (Prov. 3:5–6)

Do you think you might stress or worry less if you practiced giving
    your cares to Jesus more—and practiced reminding yourself
    more often that he truly cares for you?

Cast all your anxiety on him because he cares for you. (1 Pet. 5:7)

Do you think you might be better at staying on the path God has
    for you if you made a regular practice of reading God's Word?

    Your word is a lamp for my feet,
        a light on my path. (Ps. 119:105)

Do you think you might have an easier time believing this verse
    if you actually made a deliberate effort to practice honoring
    Mom and Dad regularly?

Children, obey your parents in the Lord, for this is right. "Honor
your father and mother"—which is the first commandment with a
promise—"so that it may go well with you and that you may enjoy
long life on the earth." (Eph. 6:1–3)

What other aspects of the Christian life would likely come much
    easier if you practiced them?

The truth is, I can't think of one area of our Christianity that
wouldn't be more effective if we practiced doing the right things
more often than we probably do.

Summing It Up

As we practice living the way God instructs us to in the Bible, it will become more and more natural for us to do the right things. Isn't this how we develop good habits?

And in many places, the Bible makes this one thing I'm about to say very clear. Ready? Here it is: It isn't enough to simply know what God's Word says. We must put it into practice.

> How can a young person stay on the path of purity?
> By living according to your word. (Ps. 119:9)

> Do not merely listen to the word, and so deceive yourselves. Do what it says. Anyone who listens to the word but does not do what it says is like someone who looks at his face in a mirror and, after looking at himself, goes away and immediately forgets what he looks like. But whoever looks intently into the perfect law that gives freedom, and continues in it—not forgetting what they have heard, but doing it—they will be blessed in what they do. (James 1:22–25)

"They will be blessed in what they do." That sounds like a really good thing, doesn't it? How might life be better if we put God's Word into practice?

A Special Word for Parents

If you want a little extra fun, pull up YouTube and check out the "Dude Perfect" team. They do some really crazy things—make one-in-a-million shots that only happen with lots and lots of practice. Check out this link in advance and see if this might be a way you can really drive the point home at the end of this devotional. Practice takes time and effort . . . but the end results? Totally worth it! https://www.youtube.com/watch?v=AE2FsgKoGD04

Lose the Diaper

THEME: Holding on to a grudge is sort of like wearing a dirty diaper. It gets heavy and old, and people tend to keep their distance!

═══ THINGS YOU'LL NEED ═══

☐ *Disposable diapers*, one for each of the kids plus two more. You'll use one of those extra diapers in advance, as a test. You'll need the second extra diaper for the end of the devotional. Ask around; it generally isn't hard to find people at church who will be happy to give you a couple unused diapers. Otherwise pick up a pack at the store or online (and perhaps donate the remainder to your church nursery). The bigger the size you can get, the better. Do you have access to some adult diapers? Even better.

☐ *Bucket of water*. Nothing fancy here, just something big enough to put the diapers in so they can absorb water. You can also use a sink.

Advance Prep

Take one of the diapers and put it in a bucket of water. You'll want to get a basic idea of how long it takes for the diaper to reach its maximum absorption. Generally, ten minutes is plenty of time. Armed with that information, you're ready to do this activity with the kids.

Running the Activity

Get the kids together and hand each of them a dry diaper. Tell them you want to see how much water it can absorb and compare how that changes its weight.

Invite them to stuff their diaper into the sink or bucket of water. Explain that they'll want to leave it there for a few minutes. In the meantime, you can dig right into the spiritual truth in the next section.

Teaching the Lesson

Let's start out with a few questions about diapers . . . and we'd like to get your input here.

What is the purpose of diapers? Basically, diapers are worn to keep clothes—of the one wearing the diaper and those close to that person—from getting messed up.

Diapers are generally intended for use by whom? Babies and toddlers who aren't potty-trained, or adults who no longer have mobility or control of certain bodily functions.

How often should diapers be changed? Every time they become wet or filled, right? Here's a multiple-choice question: What happens when diapers aren't changed that often?

A. A person with a dirty diaper begins to smell . . . and other people will get annoyed or try to avoid them.

B. A person with a dirty diaper ends up carrying a lot more weight around with them than they need to. If they can walk, their walk may look funny . . . more of a waddle.

C. Likely a dirty diaper will eventually slow down the person wearing it—or if left on long enough, may even make them sore.

D. All of the above.

Another multiple-choice question: What do we do with a dirty disposable diaper once it has been removed?

A. Let it dry so we can use it again.

B. Hide it in our bedroom so we can pull it out and look at it sometime.

C. Give it to a friend.

D. Throw it out.

There are some things that we just aren't meant to hold on to, and one of those is a full diaper. Another thing we're not to hold on to is a grudge. When somebody does something that hurts or bothers us—or fails to do something we expected them to do—it's pretty easy to get upset.

Getting upset is a natural reaction. When we feel we've been wronged, it's not like we make a choice to get upset. It happens fast, often without us thinking about it. But what's really important is what we do next. That's when we *do* have a choice.

If we hold on to that sense that we've been "wronged" somehow, we can get ourselves in trouble. We think about it, replaying it in our minds over and over.

- Maybe we think about how we'd like to get even, or would like to see that other person punished in some way.
- We think of more and more reasons why we're right and the other person is wrong.
- We begin to find ways to "punish" the other person. Maybe by things we say or do, or by being silent. We show them in different ways that they've wronged us.
- Often, we end up talking to friends about how we've been wronged—but not because we want their help in forgiving the person. It's more like we're trying to convince them that we have every right to be upset, and frequently it's about building allies who will join us in resenting the person we're mad at.
- This person who wronged us may become someone we talk about more and more . . . almost like we're obsessed with them.

So here are two BIG questions.

How are the reactions we just talked about similar to walking around with a dirty diaper?

What does the Bible say we should do when we've been wronged by someone?

Jesus says we're to forgive the person who offends us. That doesn't mean we automatically trust that person—or that things go back to the way they were before we were wronged. But we don't want to carry the dirty diaper of resentment around with us.

Then Peter came to Jesus and asked, "Lord, how many times shall I forgive my brother or sister who sins against me? Up to seven times?"
    Jesus answered, "I tell you, not seven times, but seventy-seven times." (Matt. 18:21–22)

Here are three things that might help you lose that diaper of resentment.

1. **Talk to your parents.** It's generally smart to talk to someone who has experienced more of life to help get a wider perspective. Remember, the goal is to get free of the resentment you're carrying so it doesn't hurt you more. In other words, you need to lose the diaper.

   > Listen to advice and accept discipline,
   >> and at the end you will be counted among the wise. (Prov. 19:20)

2. **Talk to the person who offended you.** And be sure to listen too.

> If your brother or sister sins, go and point out their fault, just between the two of you. If they listen to you, you have won them over. But if they will not listen, take one or two others along, so that "every matter may be established by the testimony of two or three witnesses." If they still refuse to listen, tell it to the church; and if they refuse to listen even to the church, treat them as you would a pagan or a tax collector. (Matt. 18:15–17)

3. **Take care of it quickly.** The longer you stew over how you've been wronged, the more you'll pay a price for walking around in that dirty diaper. Anger and resentment lead to bad things, and you have to lose them—fast. Don't sleep on it; get rid of it and *then* sleep. You'll sleep better. The Holy Spirit will help change your heart if you ask him to.

> "In your anger do not sin": Do not let the sun go down while you are still angry, and do not give the devil a foothold. (Eph. 4:26–27)

Summing It Up

It's time to check those diapers you left soaking. Have each of the kids pick one up and wrap it up with its own adhesive strips to form a football. Then have them compare the weight of it to the one diaper you didn't soak.

If you can, take the kids outside and have them play catch for a minute or two with the diaper footballs. Then rein it in to sum things up.

- If your diaper was filled with waste instead of water, you surely wouldn't want to be wearing it or tossing it around like a football with others.
- You wouldn't hide it in your room until it got even more ripe. You'd get rid of the diaper.
- If we walk around in a dirty diaper—and refuse to change it because we think we have every right to wear that thing—we'll find people just don't want to be all that close to us. They'll think we're a little weird too.
- If we walk around in a dirty diaper, we'll eventually get skin sores that will hurt us even more. And when we hold on to resentment or grudges, we're disobeying what Jesus taught, and that will always hurt us more in the long run.

Is there someone you resent right now? Lose the diaper.

And the next time you're tempted to hold a grudge, remember to think of it as a dirty diaper . . . and let it go.

Fuel on the Fire

THEME: We often have the power to flare up the tension between friends or family—or calm things down.

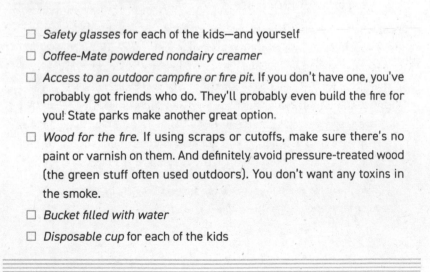

⚠ THINGS YOU'LL NEED

- ☐ *Safety glasses* for each of the kids—and yourself
- ☐ *Coffee-Mate powdered nondairy creamer*
- ☐ *Access to an outdoor campfire or fire pit.* If you don't have one, you've probably got friends who do. They'll probably even build the fire for you! State parks make another great option.
- ☐ *Wood for the fire.* If using scraps or cutoffs, make sure there's no paint or varnish on them. And definitely avoid pressure-treated wood (the green stuff often used outdoors). You don't want any toxins in the smoke.
- ☐ *Bucket filled with water*
- ☐ *Disposable cup* for each of the kids

Advance Prep

Remember, this is an outdoor activity. Don't use an indoor fireplace for this. You'll be pouring Coffee-Mate onto a fire, which will cause a dramatic flare-up of flame.

You'll want to test this before doing it with the kids. Not that it is difficult, but if you do it once you'll know what to expect and can make important adjustments, such as knowing how far your kids should stand from the flame when pouring the Coffee-Mate, how much to pour at a time, and how high the Coffee-Mate container should be held over the fire when pouring. I'll tell you this: you want to keep a good distance between the fire and the Coffee-Mate. Hold that container high. The powder will cause the fire to flare dramatically, so if your hand is too close, you may singe some hair.

A Special Word for Parents

Parents, be sure you're praying and doing a little examining of your own life before teaching this lesson.

Often, when it comes to pressing buttons, parents are masters of it—even when they don't realize they're doing it. As you're looking at your life, if you see how you might be doing this with your kids, you'll want to confess that to the family—and ask God to help you do much, much better in that area. Now, if you're thinking, *I don't have that problem* . . . can I encourage you to ask your spouse—and your kids—if you do or don't? If you have teenagers, you can be almost sure there are things you do that cause them to be frustrated. If you get some honest feedback, be careful not to get defensive. Listen. And ask the Holy Spirit to help you.

Fathers, do not exasperate your children; instead, bring them up in the training and instruction of the Lord. (Eph. 6:4)

Running the Activity

1. Ideally, build your fire twenty or thirty minutes before you plan to have the devotional. You want that fire to be well established so it has really taken hold of the wood burning there.

2. Once you have a good fire, get the kids together and have them put on safety glasses. Whenever you have your kids put on safety glasses, you're likely to get them to listen better. They get the idea that they're about to do something dangerous or something that really shouldn't be done.

3. Have them shake some Coffee-Mate on the fire. Keep a safe distance. Remember, you don't want them shaking out the powder with their hand close to the fire. The flames will surge right up and give them a high five. They'll drop the container of Coffee-Mate on the fire—and you may find yourself teaching an entirely different lesson.

4. The fire should flare up, even burning the powder still in the air. I'd let each of the kids get a chance to pour a little Coffee-Mate if they'd like to.

Now, you may have kids who want to do this over and over. I'd suggest you tell them they can have more turns—after the lesson. If they spend too much time playing with the fire ahead of your teaching time, they may begin to lose interest sooner than you'd like.

Teaching the Lesson

The things we did with the fire are like life in some ways. When we are with family or friends, things we say or do can either stir up flames of tension or conflict or calm things down.

Let's brainstorm. What kinds of things can we do to family or friends that can stir up conflict, anger, or tension between us?

When we know someone well, we know where their "buttons" or "bruises" are. We know those areas they're extra sensitive about, and if we bring up those issues, we're likely to see them react in not-so-good ways. Sometimes we press on those places because we want to make them squirm a bit, right?

We've just brainstormed ways we can provoke anger or conflict with family or friends. How many of those ways have to do with the things we say to them or about them?

- **Often, we stir up old issues, add fuel to the fire, and sometimes really grind our knuckles in the bruise.** Like when we used the Coffee-Mate, something we say or do can cause an instant flare-up of anger. Instead of calming conflict between us and others, we stir it up.

- **Is that who we really want to be? Is that who God wants us to be?** I don't think so.

> For as churning cream produces butter,
>   and as twisting the nose produces blood,
>   so stirring up anger produces strife. (Prov. 30:33)

- **This verse makes some obvious statements.** Churning butter makes cream. Wringing someone's nose is going to result in blood. And, just as true, when we press each other's buttons and poke those bruises—those sensitive areas—we're going to cause problems for them and us.

The tongue also is a fire, a world of evil among the parts of the body. It corrupts the whole body, sets the whole course of one's life on fire, and is itself set on fire by hell. (James 3:6)

The things we say to and about others can do tremendous damage to them—and to our relationship with them. Is that what we want?

Summing It Up

Let's each take a cup, fill it with water, and splash it on the base of the fire. We have the power to keep a fire of conflict going with others—or make it die out.

> A gentle answer turns away wrath,
> but a harsh word stirs up anger. (Prov. 15:1)

This is a great verse, and often gives us the secret to calming a fire down.

- We can do so when we talk nice and are considerate of another's feelings.
- We can also do so when we don't raise our voices and argue. Often, when we resist this urge, we avoid the anger and conflict we would've caused otherwise.

Let's work on that as a family: to be more thoughtful and to be nicer in the way we talk to each other. And let's see if that doesn't make our home life that much better, okay?

Instead of tossing fuel on the fire, let's use our words and our tone (the way we say things) to put out the flames that hurt others and ourselves.

Bridge Builders

THEME: Building bridges to those who are distant from us—or isolated from others—and seeing the "unseen" and reaching out to them.

THINGS YOU'LL NEED

☐ *Chairs, benches, boards, anything you can use to create a "bridge" that your kids can walk across.* Nothing fancy, just something they can walk on that will keep their feet from touching the ground. You'll want as many of these bridge-building items as you can get. The longer the bridge you can build, the better.

Advance Prep

There is nothing to do in advance, other than maybe round up some extra folding chairs or other bridge-building materials. And think of a place you'd like to do this activity. Inside the house works fine. Hopefully you'll make a bridge that goes from one room to another. Outside is great too. Again, think *long* for your bridge.

Running the Activity

Determine where you're going to set up your bridge, indoors or outdoors, and get the kids together. Set up a spot to be the "island." Maybe it's in another room—or in the neighbor's yard. One of the kids will be sent to the island, and the rest will have to rescue them . . . by building a bridge.

Explain they can use chairs, boards, benches, blankets (if you want), or anything else to build the bridge. But it must allow them to get to the person stranded on the island without stepping on the ground.

Next, the kids will go through the house or garage getting chairs or whatever else you've lined up for them to use as building blocks. They'll have to arrange these things close enough that they can walk on the bridge, stepping from chair to chair or bench all the way out to the island.

When they get to the island, and only then, the stranded person is allowed off the island and can now return with the others, using the bridge.

Once the stranded person has been rescued, you're ready to transition into a life lesson.

Teaching the Lesson

Building a bridge and rescuing the stranded one was fun, and there is a reminder here about life: sometimes other people become isolated somehow.

- Maybe it's somebody we hardly know.
- Maybe the person seems to be a loner and doesn't have friends, or not many.
- Maybe it's a family member or a friend who seems distant.

The thing is, often that distant, isolated person doesn't seem to be able to change their situation. Sometimes God wants us to build a bridge to them. In Matthew 18, Jesus talks about the Good Shepherd. Instead of just hanging with the main flock of sheep, this shepherd noticed one of the sheep wasn't there—but should have been. The missing sheep had been part of the group at one time but now was gone.

> What do you think? If a man owns a hundred sheep, and one of them wanders away, will he not leave the ninety-nine on the hills and go to look for the one that wandered off? And if he finds it, truly I tell you, he is happier about that one sheep than about the ninety-nine that did not wander off. In the same way your Father in heaven is not willing that any of these little ones should perish. (vv. 12–14)

The Good Shepherd didn't wait for the isolated sheep to find its own way back. He went out looking for it. He made an effort to reach out to the sheep—he built a bridge, in a sense, and brought the sheep home.

How was the sheep better off after Jesus brought it back?

Summing It Up

In that one story, Jesus demonstrated that sometimes we need to go out of our way for someone who is isolated or distant. We need to make an effort to bring them back—even if we were never great friends with them.

How can we be more aware of those who are isolated, lack friends, or seem more distant than they were at one time?

Is there someone who comes to mind who used to be part of your youth group but no longer comes?

How can you find a way to build a bridge to them? How can you find a way to go to that person's world or meet them where they're at right now?

Can you brainstorm some ways to reach out?

The story Jesus told ends in such a good way. The lost sheep was saved and enjoyed the care and protection of the Good Shepherd and the companionship of the other sheep.

If we're followers of Jesus, we want to be doing the same type of things as he did. We want to develop eyes that see the lonely, hurting, isolated, and lost—and growing a heart to help is part of being a follower of Jesus.

So let's be bridge builders, with God's help. Who is he impressing on your mind right now? Let's follow in Jesus's steps and do exactly what the Good Shepherd did for that lost sheep.

Escalator Epiphany

THEME: If we aren't constantly climbing in the Christian life, likely the world will pull us down.

THINGS YOU'LL NEED

☐ *Access to an escalator.* Find one at a local mall, airport (they are often in areas you can access without having to go through TSA security), large office building, or big department store.

Advance Prep

No advance prep needed other than to scope out a good escalator— and a time when there isn't much traffic flow on it.

Running the Activity

Take the kids to the escalator—and you want the one that is traveling *down*.

1. Have one—or all of the kids together—take a turn riding down the escalator.
2. Now have each of them do it a second time, individually. Tell them that this time you'll do it differently. When they are about halfway down, you'll signal to them to walk up the escalator instead. Their goal is not to simply stay in place (not going down or moving up) but rather to walk fast and hard enough to make it all the way to the top of the down escalator.
3. Now, if somebody else gets on the escalator while one of your kids is climbing the wrong way, likely they'll have to ride to the bottom and start over. If that happens, you'll use that experience in the teaching time.

After you've finished the escalator exercise, take the kids someplace where you can debrief a bit. A fast-food place is always a great choice. Get the kids ice cream, or fries and something to drink. Now their hands are busy while you talk with them. I find it's easier to get a discussion going over food. It seems to me that Jesus had some really great talks with people when there was food around too.

Teaching the Lesson

It wasn't tremendously hard to walk up the down escalator, was it? But you definitely had to stick with it. If you stopped moving, you'd start going down—fast!

Going the wrong way on the escalator is a picture of the Christian life in some ways. Any idea what I might mean by this?

Let's imagine that the escalator is the broad path that "leads to destruction" (Matt. 7:13). It represents the direction all humankind is going unless they are saved through faith in Jesus Christ. People simply seem content to ride that escalator through life, rarely thinking about where the path they're on will lead them.

As Christians, we're not to be conformed to the world. We're to be unique. In many ways, we take a very different view of what is right and wrong than our culture does. And often we're to deliberately go in a different direction than the world is going.

> Therefore, I urge you, brothers and sisters, in view of God's mercy, to offer your bodies as a living sacrifice, holy and pleasing to God—this is your true and proper worship. Do not conform to the pattern of this world, but be transformed by the renewing of your mind. Then you will be able to test and approve what God's will is—his good, pleasing and perfect will. (Rom. 12:1–2)

What are some examples of ways that Christians are to be different from those who do not follow Christ?

What happened on the escalator whenever you slowed down or stopped climbing?

How is that similar to the Christian life? What happens when we do not deliberately make an effort to climb?

If someone else got on the escalator and wanted to go down while you were climbing, you had to stop—or go down and start over. How might that be a picture of what happens with some of our friends or others we meet?

How can others slow—or stop—our climb?

How can others influence us to go backward?

Summing It Up

An epiphany is a moment when we suddenly understand something in a way we didn't before. We see something in a new light. To me, a simple escalator ride became an "epiphany moment" when I compared it to the Christian life.

In the Old Testament, there are many stories of leaders who totally messed up. King Rehoboam (Solomon's son) was one of those leaders who did pretty good overall during his first few years as king. He was climbing. Deliberately doing the right things. But eventually he messed up and went down the escalator, so to speak. Check out this revealing verse.

> He did evil because he had not set his heart on seeking the LORD. (2 Chron. 12:14)

Rehoboam's downfall was that he stopped climbing. He didn't keep his eyes focused on consistently following God. And the moment we stop following, the world pulls us down.

So there is the challenge for us. We don't want to end up going backward. We don't want to be influenced by the world. And the key is to stay focused on seeking God. We need to keep working at it and keep climbing. We deliberately purpose to do the right things—just the way the Bible teaches us to. And the good news? We don't have to do this all on our own. God will help us if we ask him to, right?

The Start or the Finish?

THEME: How we start is important, but how we finish matters most.

THINGS YOU'LL NEED

No supplies needed for this one!

Advance Prep

You're going to lead the kids in a game of Simon Says. It's probably been a really long time since you've played it, so go to YouTube and pull up an example of someone playing the game. And if you think you remember the game just fine, still check it out online. You'll probably get some great ideas for how to do it better.

Your objective is to get the kids to mess up in some way. Either they make a move without the "Simon says" preceding the instruction, or you are able to trick them into making the wrong move. For example, you might say "Simon says touch your nose"—but as the leader you simply point at your nose. If one of the kids points at their nose instead of touching it, you got them!

Running the Activity

Get the kids together and announce you'll be playing Simon Says. Review the rules. If you have teenagers who are groaning at this point, just ask them to play along. Explain that you want to see if they can actually *do* this kids' game or if they'll mess up. Tell them they just have to follow the Simon Says instructions for a couple of minutes to be considered a winner in the game. Make this fun!

If two parents are available, one can run the activity while the other plays right along with the kids. Seeing a parent mess up will make it that much more fun for the kids.

Remember, don't run the activity long. A couple of minutes should be plenty. You don't want anyone getting bored. If you get them to mess up, even if it is only one of the kids, that's all you need.

To increase your chances of getting them to mess up, you'll want to go fast. "Simon says do this. Simon says do that." Rapid fire is a key to getting them to miss. And then, of course, there's the old trick of demonstrating something different from what you're saying or dropping the "Simon says" in the middle of a quick succession of commands.

Teaching the Lesson

How we started the game was important. All of you were listening. Paying attention. You knew you had to follow my instructions exactly—but only if I said "Simon says" first. So all of you started the game really, really well.

But in order to win, it really mattered how you finished. If you kept following the instructions and didn't get fooled, you would win.

In life, what do you think God is most concerned about: how we start things, or how we finish?

Listen to a story Jesus told:

"What do you think? There was a man who had two sons. He went to the first and said, 'Son, go and work today in the vineyard.'

"'I will not,' he answered, but later he changed his mind and went.

"Then the father went to the other son and said the same thing. He answered, 'I will, sir,' but he did not go.

"Which of the two did what his father wanted?"

"The first," they answered. (Matt. 21:28–31)

One son started by saying the right things . . . he started well, but he didn't finish well. His good start didn't count. It was how he finished that really mattered.

The other son started horribly but later did the right thing. His bad start didn't disqualify him some way. It was how he finished that mattered most.

The same is true in our spiritual life. We can say all the right things about wanting to be a disciple of Jesus. We can say we want to obey the commands and principles God gives in the Bible. But what really matters is if we actually do it . . . and keep doing it throughout our life.

There's a bizarre story in 1 Kings 13 in the Old Testament about a man who was sent by God to deliver a message to wicked King Jeroboam. It was a dangerous mission, because the message he was to bring was not one the king would like. Jeroboam could have ordered that the messenger be killed.

But the man obeyed God, despite the obvious danger. He followed each of the instructions God gave, and he delivered the message. However, his mission wasn't over. God then made it clear to him that he was to go home by a different route—and not eat or drink anything until he was no longer in King Jeroboam's kingdom.

While on his way home, this man of God was approached by a stranger who claimed to be a man of God as well. The stranger said an angel instructed him to meet the messenger and bring him home for a meal. The stranger was lying to him, but the man of God fell for the trick.

The story ends badly. The man of God who had obeyed so well at the start didn't finish well. He failed to complete the mission. He did not obey the full instructions from God but got derailed into disobeying based on the smooth talk of a stranger. As a result, the man of God who had started out so well lost his life.

Summing It Up

As Christians, it can be pretty easy to get off to a good start. We're obeying God and his Word. Terrific! But we must be careful to keep going. You can be sure that the enemy will try to trick you into getting sidetracked.

Maybe you feel you've already messed up. But like the first son in the story Jesus told, even if you have a bad start, you can turn that around. Confess it to God and start obeying him, doing what he wants you to do.

How we start is important, sure. But over and over and over in the Bible we see that the most important thing is how we finish.

Be a Bozo

THEME: The importance of persevering with a good attitude—even with a smile on our face—when facing unkind words or actions, even in our own family.

THINGS YOU'LL NEED

☐ *Inflatable bop bag—ideally, one with a smiling face.* Personally, I chose a 46-inch Bozo the Clown bop bag, and it was under $20 online.

Advance Prep

All you'll need to do is inflate that bop bag. Now, backhand that clown right across the chops. It should rock over on its side—and come right back to an upright position. If it isn't righting itself, try adding more air.

Running the Activity

Give each of the kids a chance to whack the bop bag a couple times. Nothing too crazy. Generally, an easy backhand hit is plenty to illustrate the point—and to be sure the bop bag doesn't get destroyed.

Teaching the Lesson

Sometimes it's easy to get irritated with someone, even right here in our family. And sometimes we can show our annoyance or frustration by taking a "shot" at another family member somehow.

Hopefully we don't physically hit/hurt that person in any way. But what are some other ways we might lash out at someone we're supposed to love?

- Saying something unkind, nasty, rude, or hurtful to that person.
- Treating that person meanly in some way.

Now, when we get treated poorly by someone like that, how do we tend to react?

Do we say something unkind, nasty, or rude right back?

Do we treat that person meanly in some way to get even or give them a taste of their own medicine?

Think about that clown bop bag for a moment. No matter how many times we hit the clown, he always came back smiling. Did you notice that?

- He never hit back.
- He never even said something nasty to you.

In some ways, that's how we should be as Christians, even if others aren't treating us right. Let's take a look at some verses from Romans 12.

Bless those who persecute you; bless and do not curse. (v. 14)

Live in harmony with one another. (v. 16)

Do not repay anyone evil for evil. Be careful to do what is right in the eyes of everyone. If it is possible, as far as it depends on you, live at peace with everyone. (vv. 17–18)

We live in a world where people are quick to demand their rights, demand justice, and often demand payback. This "world mentality" doesn't fit well with so much of the teaching of the Bible—as the verses above point out. Would you agree with that?

In fact, Jesus gave some pretty clear instructions of what we're to do if we've been wronged.

So watch yourselves. If your brother or sister sins against you, rebuke them; and if they repent, forgive them. Even if they sin against you seven times in a day and seven times come back to you saying "I repent," you must forgive them. (Luke 17:3–4)

So if you feel you've been treated wrong by someone, it's okay to call them out on it. That's what the word "rebuke" in the verses above is all about. But rebuking isn't about treating others meanly or rudely right back. And Jesus talks about us having patience with others too.

When somebody wrongs us, while Jesus instructs us to forgive so we don't grow bitter, that doesn't mean we are obligated to trust that person. Sometimes we forgive but also realize the other person is not "safe" for us, and we need to keep our distance. Can you think of an example?

How do you think life—even family life—would be different if we were quick to forgive when we are wronged by what someone does or says?

A Special Word for Parents

This might be a good time to remind the kids that the principles of this lesson are not intended to apply to situations where some form of physical/verbal abuse is taking place. Whether abuse is coming from family, friends, leaders, or others, Scripture doesn't support allowing that abuse to continue. Talk to the kids about the topic. I know parents who had no idea their son or daughter was being abused until the damage was deep. Make sure your kids know that they can always talk to you about the topic—and should.

Summing It Up

Think about how we react to friends and family—and how we could react. Imagine living according to what the Bible teaches:

- Not giving a nasty comeback when someone says something nasty to us.
- Not seeking some kind of vengeance when someone wrongs us.
- Forgiving others when we haven't been treated well and they ask for forgiveness.

God can help us do exactly that. He'll help us if we ask, and he's given us his Holy Spirit to make that all possible.

And if we live that way—treating people nicely even when they aren't nice to us—some people may think we're a real clown. They may see us as a total bozo to "let others get away with how they're treating you." But I want to encourage you: when you do the right things, there are even more payoffs.

> Consider it pure joy, my brothers and sisters, whenever you face trials of many kinds, because you know that the testing of your faith produces perseverance. Let perseverance finish its work so that you may be mature and complete, not lacking anything. (James 1:2–4)

Not that we have to be like that inflatable bop bag, coming back for more abuse . . . but let's keep coming back to love that person, with a smile on our face!

Concrete Shoes

THEME: The longer we wait to step away from sin, the harder it is to break free.

THINGS YOU'LL NEED

- ☐ *5-gallon plastic bucket or pail.* These should be $5 or under at most hardware stores. You can get one bucket—or, to make the illustration more personal, pick up a bucket for each of the kids.
- ☐ *Bag of ordinary concrete mix.* It may come in a 60- or 80-pound bag, so be careful.
- ☐ *Stir stick to mix cement.* One for each pail would be nice. A small gardening shovel or even a broom handle works fine.
- ☐ *An old shoe for each of the kids, if possible.* The shoes will be ruined in the end, so bear that in mind. Don't have old shoes? Check the thrift store nearest you—or family and friends.
- ☐ *Optional: strong box cutter/utility knife*
- ☐ *Optional: heat gun.* Check with neighbors or friends to see if you can borrow one.

If borrowing tools . . . put your thumb in this page and flip back to page 27 to give **Borrowing Supplies Is a Good Thing—If You Do It Right** a quick skim. Get this right and you'll gain respect . . . and an open door to borrow tools again. You'll also teach your kids how to do it right.

Advance Prep

Read the mixing instructions on the bag of cement. You can do a test run of this in advance, or, because it takes some real effort, mix it for the first time when you're doing it with the kids.

You'll want to choose a place to do this activity outside, with access to a water hose. Another good reason to do this outdoors? It's going to get messy.

One more thing. Ideally, you'll do this devotional over the course of two different days. The first time you get together, you'll do the activity described in the section immediately below. Then, a day or two later, after the cement has hardened, you'll finish by teaching the lesson.

Running the Activity

Have a bucket for each of the kids with about six inches of cement powder at the bottom. Let the kids mix their own bucket of cement, if possible. You'll want to add water sparingly. It is better to add a smaller amount of water at a time than to have too much water. You don't want the cement to be too soupy, or it will take forever to set.

1. Add water (or more concrete mix) as needed until the consistency is smooth, like mashed potatoes.
2. Have the kids put on an old shoe and step that foot into the bucket so the shoe sinks down into the wet cement. You want

their shoe deep enough for the cement to close in over the toe of the shoe but not so deep that the shoe is completely buried. You don't want cement to come high enough to ooze into the shoe.

3. Now, have them lift their foot—and the shoe they're wearing—out of the cement. It should be fairly easy to do.

4. So far, so good . . . you're almost done. Now have them put their foot right back into the cement like they did the first time. Be sure the shoe is buried deep enough in the cement that the top of the shoe and a majority of the laces are fully covered this time.

5. Finally, have them untie their laces and slip their foot out of the shoe—leaving the shoe behind in the bucket of cement. It's important that no cement drops into the shoe itself.

6. Put those buckets aside where that cement will harden.

You're all set for today. Tell the kids you're doing this lesson in two parts, but resist the urge to tell them what comes next—or the point of the lesson. Let them guess all they want, but if you keep an element of mystery they'll anticipate the devotion that much more.

Make sure the cement has hardened fully before teaching the lesson.

Teaching the Lesson

When the cement was wet, on a scale of one to ten, with ten being the hardest, how tough was it to pull your foot out of the bucket while still wearing the shoe?

1. I'd like you to go to your bucket, slip your shoe back on your foot, and tie the laces.

2. Okay, once your shoe is on tight, try walking around with the bucket on your foot.

3. Now, pull your foot out of the bucket—shoe and all. One to ten, how hard is it to remove your foot now?

This illustrates a truth about life. Sometimes we get involved in sin, doing something that the Bible tells us is wrong. We step right into it. Like pulling our foot out of the wet cement, freeing ourselves from sin can be messy, but with God's help we can do it. Yet there is an important key . . . a principle to freeing ourselves from sin: *we need to get out of it quickly*. And here's why:

- The longer we allow ourselves to walk in sin, the more it will slow us down until we do get free.
- The longer we allow ourselves to walk in sin, the tougher it will be to get free from it. Sin has a way of hardening us and getting a grip on us that gets increasingly hard to pull away from.

Check out this Scripture.

Therefore, since we are surrounded by such a great cloud of witnesses, let us throw off everything that hinders and the sin that so easily entangles. And let us run with perseverance the race marked out for us, fixing our eyes on Jesus, the pioneer and perfecter of faith. (Heb. 12:1–2)

Sin entangles us quickly . . . like the way our shoe sunk so easily into that wet cement. The sooner we break free, the sooner we confess our sin and turn away from it, the better off we'll be.

God has a plan for our lives. A race for us to run. We aren't going to be effective with the weight of sin slowing us down.

Summing It Up

We all step into sin. Unforgiveness. Selfishness. Anger. Dishonesty. Unkind talk. Pride. Worry. The list goes on.

> Do you feel like maybe you're weighed down with some sin right now? Something that is keeping you from running that race Jesus has marked out for you?
>
> Is there anything you need to confess now—to God, to a brother or sister, or to me?

Optional: remove the concrete from the bucket with the kids. You may be able to loosen it by standing the pail upside down on the ground and giving it a friendly thump. If that doesn't work, use a heat gun to warm the plastic and then cut the bucket off with a utility knife. The plastic will cut like butter once it's heated. Now the shoe set in concrete can be displayed in the corner of your kid's room as a reminder of the need to break free from sin—fast.

The Things We Miss When We Have Our Nose to the Phone

THEME: Too much screen time—like being on our phones—causes us to miss things. There are rewards to being more present and engaged wherever we're at, rather than focused on a screen.

THINGS YOU'LL NEED

- [ ] *A smartphone for each of the kids to use.* If they don't have phones (yay!) they can just borrow yours when it is their turn to run the race (or see sidebar below for another option).
- [ ] *An envelope for each of the kids with their name on it.* You'll want to put this somewhere on the route you'll map out for the kids to run. In the envelope can be a note for a "gift certificate" of sorts. Tailor each note to the child . . . something age appropriate that they'd really like. Some examples:

Permission to stay up one hour later.

Permission to stay out one hour later.

Take them out to eat to the restaurant of their choice.

Make their favorite dessert or meal sometime in the next week.

For the next family movie night, they get to pick the movie.

Or you may want to slip $5 in the envelope . . . or $20.

Advance Prep

1. Line up a "course" that the kids will run. It can be a route through the house or outside. Either works fine.

2. Get the envelopes ready for each of the kids.

3. Hide the envelopes. Here's the thing. You'll want to be fair and put the envelopes where they can be seen. But what we're hoping for is that they'll *miss* the envelope because they're too busy texting. So keep that in mind when you're hiding the envelopes along the route. Make it someplace they likely won't see if they're texting—but will see if they're not.

Phones are expensive . . . and if the kids aren't at an age where you want them doing an activity with your phone, I get it! If that's the case, swap out the phone for anything that will occupy their attention. A great alternative would be one of those flashing safety lights made to mount on bikes. If you use this, have them count the number of flashes aloud while they're doing the obstacle course. This will still get the point across that being on a phone will distract them more than they realize. For the sake of consistency, we'll write the rest of the lesson as if you're using the phone—but remember the light works just as easily. Whether you use a phone or a flashing light to teach this lesson, you'll still tie it in exactly the same way.

Running the Activity

Explain the activity to the kids.

1. They'll run the obstacle course—but they must fire off texts to you the entire time. They can't fire off a few texts and then run the course. They should be sending out a running stream of texts.
2. Tell them the winner isn't just the fastest person. You will also be counting how many texts you get from them. Every text can take a second off their time, so if one kid finishes the course in 45 seconds and sends 10 texts, their score is 35. If another kid crosses the finish line in 48 seconds but sent 14 texts to you, their score is 34. Even though they finished second, they pull first place. (If you're using the bike light, you can take ten seconds off their time if you never hear them miss a count as they numbered the flashes aloud.)
3. Have each kid run the course and figure out the scores to see who won.

If nobody found their envelope, you're in a great spot to teach the lesson.

Teaching the Lesson

I want to read you a story from the life of Jesus, and while it doesn't perfectly illustrate what I'd like to talk about today, it comes close. *Read the story of Mary and Martha in Luke 10:38–42.*

As Jesus and his disciples were on their way, he came to a village where a woman named Martha opened her home to him. She had a sister called Mary, who sat at the Lord's feet listening to what he said. But

Martha was distracted by all the preparations that had to be made. She came to him and asked, "Lord, don't you care that my sister has left me to do the work by myself? Tell her to help me!"

"Martha, Martha," the Lord answered, "you are worried and upset about many things, but few things are needed—or indeed only one. Mary has chosen what is better, and it will not be taken away from her."

We may be oversimplifying here, but notice some little things about this story.

- Mary focused on the person right there in the room with her.
- Martha focused on how she wanted others to see her.

It wasn't just that Martha didn't want to do all the work. She wanted to come off as a good hostess. She had an image to maintain. She had to appear as this person who was all things to all people—and she felt she wasn't holding it together.

How might our time on our phones, whether on social media or texting friends, be partially about maintaining our image with people who aren't even in the room with us?

Jesus pointed out that Mary, who chose to be present with the one in front of her, made the better choice. How does this apply to our screen use? Any ideas? *Note: If you used the flashing light option instead of a phone, you'll need to do a bit of transition here before going to the next question. Maybe something like "With the flashing light in your hand, it definitely stole some of your attention from what was going on around you. The same thing often happens when people have a phone with them."*

Is it possible that when others are in the room yet we focus on our screens—on people who aren't in the room—we're making a poor choice?

Is it possible that when we're on our screens we're more interested in how others see us than we are in the people right in the room with us?

Martha thought she had to do everything—or that she could somehow pull off focusing on making a meal and maintaining this image of herself as the perfect hostess while somehow also focusing on her guest. She was wrong. She was missing something.

Mary focused on Jesus—which, of course, is the absolute right thing to do. But she also demonstrated that she gave her full attention to the one in the room with her.

- She didn't try to multitask and get other work done.
- She certainly didn't try to keep up with friends who weren't there.

Mary must have known that she couldn't make a meal for a group *and* truly be present with Jesus. So she made a choice.

And we have to make a choice too. Yes, we like to keep up with friends. And often we have an image we feel we need to maintain by texting or interacting on social media. But there is a time to text and a time not to. Jesus made it clear that Mary made the better choice. I think we would do really well to learn to put our phones away when we're physically with others. Take a lesson from Mary and focus on the people who are in the room with you . . . not on those who aren't.

Martha didn't like that Mary wasn't paying attention to her, and she wanted Jesus to get Mary to respond. How do others pressure you to be on the phone texting—or on social media—on *their* schedule?

Summing It Up

When you ran the race, you were busy texting. Now, you finished the course okay. None of you fell or got lost. But could you have missed something that you might have otherwise noticed if you had not been texting?

Take them to the envelopes and show them what they missed by being so focused on their phones. They may say that you aren't being fair. They may think what you did was awful. But the truth? They're likely missing things every day because they aren't focused on who is right there in front of them.

Kids, when we text, when we spend so much time with our nose to the phone, likely we are missing things. Haven't you seen that before? Can any of you tell of a time you observed that with others?

I want to encourage you to set the phone aside when you are with real live people. Focus on *them*. If you don't, I guarantee you'll miss good things . . . and will be making a poor choice, just like Martha.

I'd put the envelopes back where they were and have the kids run the race again—but without phones this time. Let them find the envelopes and win whatever you had planned for them. This will reinforce the benefits of putting the phone aside.

Strength Sappers

THEME: Exposure to fear, worry, anxiety, or other wrong things can leave us weak and unprotected.

THINGS YOU'LL NEED

- ☐ *Raw eggs.* One for each of the kids would be good. I'd add one or two extras in case one breaks during the experiment.
- ☐ *Vinegar.* Regular household white vinegar is fine.
- ☐ *Clear glasses, jars, or bowls to soak the eggs in.* One for each of the kids would be best.

Advance Prep

This devotion takes over a full week to prep for the actual lesson, because the eggs will need to sit for days. I'd have the kids help with the prep for this so they're more invested on the day you actually teach the devo.

Running the Activity

Day 1: Have each of the kids put an egg in a clear glass or bowl. Add enough vinegar to cover every bit of the egg. Be sure the kids wash their hands well . . . eggs can have nasty bacteria on their shells.

Day 2: Carefully pour out all the vinegar from each container and replace with fresh vinegar.

Days 3–8: Let the eggs sit in that same vinegar you poured on day 2.

Day 9: Carefully pour off the vinegar. Gently rinse the shell-less egg with water. You can keep the egg in the glass, but better yet, ease it onto a plate. You might want to hold that egg up to the light so the kids can see the yoke inside. You're ready to teach the lesson.

Teaching the Lesson

The shell is all about protecting the egg, right?

- The shell protects the baby chicken growing inside when a mother hen sits on it to keep the egg warm so it can hatch.
- The shell protects the egg when it is transported to stores to sell as food.

The egg we used in our experiment no longer has its hard shell.

- The egg basically lost its protection.
- All we have left is this sack, this membrane that was inside the hard shell.

We didn't actually see the shell disappear before our eyes, but it was slowly being attacked and dissolved by the vinegar. In the Old Testament, there is the account of when the Israelites attacked the great walled city of Jericho. This city was seen as practically unbeatable because of its mighty walls. You can read the story in Joshua 5:13–6:27. God gave the Israelites unusual instructions to defeat this city.

- Instead of surrounding the city and engaging in battle, God had the army march around the city one time, then go back to their camp.
- God had them do the same thing the second day too. And the third day. Fourth. Fifth. And the sixth.
- But on the seventh day, they were to march around the city seven times, then give a mighty shout.

They followed God's instructions, and the walls of Jericho tumbled to the ground—leaving the people inside unprotected.

The Israelite army didn't destroy the walls. God did that. But in a way, God had already destroyed the walls of Jericho before they crumbled. By having the army march around the city day after day, he was dissolving the sense of protection the Jericho soldiers felt from their wall and filling them with a fresh dose of fear, worry, and anxiety each day so that they were weak and easy to conquer once those walls came down.

In fact, God had been surrounding them with fear even before the Israelites marched around the city. Listen to what Rahab, a resident of Jericho, told the Israelite spies who had come to do a little recon of the city.

Before the spies lay down for the night, she went up on the roof and said to them, "I know that the LORD has given you this land and that a great fear of you has fallen on us, so that all who live in this country are melting in fear because of you." (Josh. 2:8–9)

- Surrounded by vinegar, the egg lost its protective shell.
- Surrounded by fear, worry, and anxiety, the Jericho soldiers lost their courage to fight—even before their wall crumbled.

The story of Jericho's defeat can teach us some important principles about life. As Christians, we have to remember that we also can be weakened by whatever surrounds us.

Worry, anxiety, and fear weaken our faith, leaving us unprotected like that egg without a shell.

Scientifically, there is a reason the vinegar dissolved the protective eggshell. There's a formula. And Christians have a formula too.

Exposure to WORRY, FEAR, or ANXIETY + TIME = WEAKER FAITH and UNPROTECTED CHRISTIANS

The soldiers in Jericho couldn't escape the fear that ate away at them. Running from fear, worry, or anxiety—or attempting to bury it—never works for long. Instead of running from whatever is eating at us like that, we need to run to Jesus and throw our worries on him.

Cast all your anxiety on him because he cares for you. (1 Pet. 5:7)

> Cast your cares on the LORD
>   and he will sustain you;
> he will never let
>   the righteous be shaken. (Ps. 55:22)

Do not be anxious about anything, but in every situation, by prayer and petition, with thanksgiving, present your requests to God. (Phil. 4:6)

Summing It Up

If the egg had a brain and realized the vinegar bath was going to eat away every bit of its protective armor, I imagine it would have tried to get away. (Of course, it would have needed arms and legs along with that brain too.)

But *we* have brains. We have arms and legs. Are we exposing ourselves to anyone or anything that will weaken us as Christians? Let's use our brains—and our arms and legs—to get out of that situation.

Is our faith being weakened by worry, anxiety, or fear? We need to ask God to help us with that before we end up as unprotected and weak as this shell-less egg!

A Special Word for Parents

If your kids are struggling with fear, worry, or anxiety, stay with this. Keep checking on them throughout the next days and weeks. Take them to the Bible to help them see what God says about these issues. Then walk your kids through how to trust him in their situation.

Take Me to Your Leader

THEME: Choosing wisely who we follow and who we shouldn't. We want our kids to be leaders, but God wired us to be followers too. Great leaders know who to follow . . . and who to avoid.

THINGS YOU'LL NEED

☐ *The family car.* You'll be taking a drive together. Also, you may want to coordinate this with a friend. See the note in the Running the Activity section below.

Advance Prep

No prep needed, although it would be really, really good to think through this whole issue of your kids being leaders or followers before teaching this lesson.

Often parents talk about the need for their kids to be leaders. What they're really saying is that they fear others may have a bad influence on their kids. They're hoping that if their kids are leaders, they'll stand strong and not be negatively influenced by anyone else. They're hoping their kids will make good choices and do the right things.

Remember, God created us to be followers. He wired us that way. We're called to be followers of God, right? We're told to follow Jesus. So being a follower is a good and needed thing. The important thing is not so much that our kids have to be leaders. Rather, they have to make good choices about who they follow.

And the truth is, not all of our kids were designed to be leaders. But God destined every one of our kids to learn to follow. If our kids are leaders, terrific. We can train them to be good ones. But all of our kids must learn to follow. And that starts with choosing the right people to follow.

Even leaders must be followers. They follow someone higher in rank. Or maybe they follow a hero from the past. I imagine some leaders have followed only their own selfish passions or agendas—in other words, they were following themselves. Which probably made them lousy leaders. Whether a person becomes a good leader or not often depends on who they follow.

So wishing for our kids to be leaders is not the answer—because not all leaders are good. Let's focus on helping our kids make good decisions about who to follow.

Running the Activity

For this devo, you're going to take the kids for a drive in the car. Ask one of them to choose a car to follow. Then do your best to follow—safely. If the lead car pulls into a parking lot, gas station, or restaurant, you do the same. If the car you're following seems a bit boring, feel free to choose a new one.

If possible, do this around a mealtime. Why? It would be powerful if the car you're following pulled into a fast-food drive-thru. When you get to the ordering spot, simply ask them to duplicate the order of the car in front of you. Then when you pick up the order, you'll have the fun and chaos of dividing the spoils.

> If you want to make sure this happens, coordinate this ahead of time with a friend. Set up a rendezvous time and place so you can follow them right into a fast-food drive-thru lane.

After a short time of following another car (five minutes is usually enough; you don't want the kids to get bored), I'd go to a fast-food place and get a meal or a snack for the kids—if you didn't follow a car into a drive-thru.

Teaching the Lesson

Everybody follows somebody . . . even if it is only their own selfish wants or desires.

Who does the "top dog" at a corporation follow?
Who does the president of the United States follow?

God made us to be followers. But who or what do we follow?

1. God/Jesus/the Holy Spirit
2. The Bible
3. People who are faithfully following number 1 and number 2

Let's look at each of these quickly.

Following God

It is the LORD your God you must follow, and him you must revere. Keep his commands and obey him; serve him and hold fast to him. (Deut. 13:4)

Following Jesus

While he was still speaking, a bright cloud covered them, and a voice from the cloud said, "This is my Son, whom I love; with him I am well pleased. Listen to him!" (Matt. 17:5)

God told the disciples to listen to Jesus, which is all about doing what Jesus says or following him. It is important to remember that God desires us to follow Jesus. Many times in the Gospels, Jesus told people to follow him too.

Then he said to them all: "Whoever wants to be my disciple must deny themselves and take up their cross daily and follow me." (Luke 9:23)

Following the Holy Spirit

Since we live by the Spirit, let us keep in step with the Spirit. (Gal. 5:25)

Following the Bible

All Scripture is God-breathed and is useful for teaching, rebuking, correcting and training in righteousness, so that the servant of God may be thoroughly equipped for every good work. (2 Tim. 3:16–17)

Following People Who Are Faithful Followers

Whatever you have learned or received or heard from me, or seen in me—put it into practice. And the God of peace will be with you. (Phil. 4:9)

A great test to know if someone is worth following is to ask these two questions:

> Are they following God/Jesus/the Holy Spirit not just by what they say but by the evidence you see in their life?
>
> Are they following the Bible and actually doing what the Bible tells us to do?

What if you must follow a person who fails that test? A boss. A teacher. A coach. There are people we must follow at times—even if they are not faithful followers themselves. We must be aware that they may lead us down a wrong path and be careful that following them doesn't cause us to disobey what Jesus taught or what the Bible says.

Summing It Up

There are many, many people we can follow. Not all of them will lead us to a good place. Not all of them will lead us in the direction Christ wants us to go. Not all of them will lead us to become the kind of people God wants us to be.

You don't have to be a "leader" to live the life that God created you to live. You just have to make wise choices about who you follow. That's one of the marks of a great leader anyway!

Holy Howling Hex Nut

THEME: The importance of listening to that voice inside us—even when we don't understand it or it scares us.

THINGS YOU'LL NEED

☐ *Balloons.* One for each of the kids—and yourself, of course. The typical classic teardrop shape. You'll want good quality balloons, so forget about buying them from the dollar store. Look for a better balloon, often advertised as being "helium quality." They'll be a little thicker than the cheapo balloons. You can find them online or at a party store. The balloons should inflate to about 12 inches—and it will state that fact on the bag.

☐ *Hex nuts.* The six-sided nuts you'd use to snug down a bolt. I used one that fit a 5/16-inch bolt, and it worked great. Get one hex nut for each of the kids.

☐ *Safety glasses* for everyone present

☐ *A place outside* to do this, far from any windows

Advance Prep

You'll definitely want to test this in advance, and it won't take you five minutes. But they'll be five minutes well spent—and I'll bet you'll be smiling in the end.

Now, before you get into practicing the activity, remember to read through the teaching part of this lesson in advance too. You'll see that you'll need a personal story—yours or a friend's—of when that little voice inside you warned of danger.

Ready to try the activity?

1. Take the hex nut and feed it through the opening of the balloon.

2. Inflate the balloon until it is nice and full, then tie it off with a tight knot.

3. Grab the balloon like you're palming a basketball. You'll basically cup your hand over the knotted end of the balloon, the narrowest part. Getting a grip can be a little tricky, and you don't want to squeeze the daylights out of the balloon so that it gets out of shape. So you may want to moisten your fingertips slightly or wear a pair of rubber or latex gloves for an easier grip.

4. Hold the balloon at a slight angle and rotate your arm in a circular motion. Eventually all you'll really need to move is your wrist. The idea is to get the hex nut to race around the inside of the balloon. As you build up speed, the hex nut inside will give off a spooky howling sound—louder than you'd probably expect.

Are you smiling? Told you.

KEEP IT SAFE

Safety glasses may not seem necessary, but they're important. If the balloon pops (and it will if that hex nut is whirling around inside the balloon too long), that hex nut could go flying in any direction. So safety glasses are a must—and I'd also do this one outdoors, a safe distance from any cars or windows.

Running the Activity

When the kids are together, have them put on safety glasses.

1. Now give each kid a balloon and a hex nut. Tell them that they're going to give the balloon a voice of sorts. Ask them to feed the hex nut inside and then blow up the balloon. If the kids need help with this, step in and give a hand—or have balloons for the younger kids all inflated and ready to go before you start.
2. Explain that by putting the nut inside the balloon and moving it just right, they should be able to hear spooky howling—from inside the balloon! Play this up a bit.
3. Demonstrate how to get the hex nut rolling, and let each of the kids try to get their balloon howling. If they can't seem to get it, you can step in and help, but have them keep their hand on yours so they get the feel just a bit.

Teaching the Lesson

Once the balloon got going in the right direction, how easy was it to hear the howling nut inside?

Did you know that each of us has a conscience, a voice of sorts deep inside us that helps us know what is right and wrong? Often that voice warns us of danger or lets us know when we're about to make a mistake. Do any of you have an example of when you experienced something like that?

Many times, that voice inside also reminds us when we've made a mistake by something we've said or done—especially if it resulted in us hurting someone else. Have you ever experienced that?

And Christians receive a very special voice inside them besides the "gut feeling" or conscience most people have. Anybody know what that special voice is?

And you also were included in Christ when you heard the message of truth, the gospel of your salvation. When you believed, you were marked in him with a seal, the promised Holy Spirit, who is a deposit guaranteeing our inheritance until the redemption of those who are God's possession—to the praise of his glory. (Eph. 1:13–14)

God gives us the Holy Spirit, his supernatural presence inside us, to

- teach us
- encourage us
- show us right and wrong
- warn us of danger or traps
- guide us and keep us on the right paths
- mature us as Christians . . . to make us more and more like Jesus
- produce good "fruit" in us
- help us understand God's Word

The howling hex nut might have sounded a little scary at first. But later it didn't scare you a bit. And sometimes following the Holy

A Special Word for Parents

If you have a story to share yourself, that would be powerful. Or you can talk to friends—or go online and find some stories. Even when reading stories of people who survived a brutal attack, it is amazing how often they had a "gut feeling" seconds before that warned them not to go in that elevator, or to run, or whatever. Warning them they were going someplace or doing something that was not a good idea. Often these people ignored the voice. If you have a story like that, it would really be impactful to share it with the kids.

Spirit's direction can be scary too. Sometimes the Holy Spirit will nudge us to do things that we'd rather not.

- He may prompt us to confess and say "I'm sorry" when we've done something wrong.
- Or he may prompt us to stand strong and not do something we know is wrong—even though our friends are doing it.

Summing It Up

The howling hex nut is really loud—and hard to ignore. The Holy Spirit isn't. And we generally don't hear an audible voice but rather it is more a sense we get. A feeling. We sense God leading us—especially as we read the Bible or are praying—and it's up to us to follow him.

Just like people often ignore their conscience, it's really easy to ignore that leading and prompting—the voice of the Holy Spirit inside us. The Bible calls that "quenching" the Spirit, because it's sort of like pouring water on a flame.

Do not quench the Spirit. (1 Thess. 5:19)

Do you think it is wise or smart to ignore the Spirit?

How many more hurtful mistakes do you think we might make if we quench the Spirit?

How do you think we can do better at listening to that voice inside us?

Do you think that might be a good thing to do, even at bedtime? To ask God to show us where we messed up during the day— and to let us know how to do better tomorrow—or fix what we did wrong today?

So I say, walk by the Spirit, and you will not gratify the desires of the flesh. For the flesh desires what is contrary to the Spirit, and the Spirit what is contrary to the flesh. They are in conflict with each other. (Gal. 5:16–17)

Once we got the hang of the little balloon experiment, it was really easy to hear the hex nut inside. And the more we get in the practice of asking for God's direction—and listening to what the Holy Spirit is saying—the easier it will be to sense and get a feel for what he is telling us.

Let's work on that, okay?

A Special Word for Parents

This lesson is one you'll want to follow up on. Check back with the kids in a few days. Share with them how you've felt the Holy Spirit lead you, and ask them if they've sensed the Lord leading them through that still, small voice inside them too.

Hard Work Pays Off

THEME: The Bible stresses the importance of being good workers instead of being lazy. A person who possesses a good work ethic will often be appreciated—and rewarded.

THINGS YOU'LL NEED

- ☐ *1 cup heavy cream*, available in the dairy section of the grocery store. It may also be called heavy whipping cream.
- ☐ *1 cup whole milk*
- ☐ *6 tablespoons white sugar*
- ☐ *2 teaspoons vanilla extract*
- ☐ *1 cup rock salt*, available at the grocery store. I used Morton Ice Cream Rock Salt. I wouldn't recommend using the rock salt used to melt snow on sidewalks. You don't want to risk any chemicals from snow-melting salt accidently mixing with your dessert.

- [ ] *Clean, round plastic container* (like from a large container of yogurt), or even better, a coffee can with a plastic lid. If you can get a couple different sizes, that's great. I used a sturdy, cylinder-shaped plastic storage container with a really secure lid, and it worked terrific. **You don't want the ingredients inside to fill more than half of the container.**
- [ ] *5-gallon plastic bucket with lid*, available at hardware stores.
- [ ] *Large bag of ice*, enough to fill that 5-gallon bucket. Available at grocery and convenience stores.
- [ ] *Duct tape.* Only if needed to keep the container lid in place.

Note: You'll be tempted to increase the ingredients so that you'll have more ice cream to enjoy. And that's fine, but realize if you double the recipe, you'll also need to double the time you'll be rolling that bucket around.

Advance Prep

It's usually wise to test each activity in advance, but this one is a bit more elaborate. So if you can test it ahead of time, great. If not, just be sure you've got all the supplies needed.

Running the Activity

Announce to the kids that today you're going to make ice cream—with their help. Have the kids assist as you mix the ingredients and prepare the makeshift ice cream maker.

1. Mix the cream, milk, sugar, and vanilla into the coffee can or plastic container. Remember, it should fill the container no more than halfway.
2. Put the lid on the container and use duct tape, if desired, to make it extra secure.

3. Place a layer of ice about 4 inches thick in the 5-gallon bucket, sprinkle in a bit of salt, then put the container on top of it.

4. Add a layer of ice all the way around the plastic container, sprinkling in the rock salt as you do. You'll want the ice a good 4 inches thick on all sides.

5. Fill the rest of the bucket with ice and sprinkled rock salt.

6. Put the bucket lid in place and, if needed, duct-tape it securely.

7. Now, have the kids roll the bucket around for a good thirty minutes. Set a timer. I took the handle off my 5-gallon bucket so it would roll easier, and I set two chairs about eight feet apart, facing each other. From one chair, I rolled the bucket to the person sitting in the other chair. They rolled it back. The key is that the bucket must keep moving—without popping off the lid.

8. After the thirty minutes are up (which will feel like a long time), open the bucket, remove the container inside and wipe it off, and pop off the lid.

9. Some of the ice cream inside will be more frozen than other parts, so stir with a spoon to get a nice, smooth consistency.

Congratulations, you just made ice cream! There isn't much here, so you'll want to serve it to the kids before it melts. If you do have any ice cream left over, put it in the freezer. It will make a nice treat later . . . and will be a good reminder of today's lesson.

Teaching the Lesson

Okay, that was some hard work you did, but the work paid off. Did you know the Bible says a lot about the importance of hard work?

All hard work brings a profit,
  but mere talk leads only to poverty. (Prov. 14:23)

Those who work their land will have abundant food,
  but those who chase fantasies have no sense. (12:11)

One who is slack in his work
  is brother to one who destroys. (18:9)

Did you catch some of the things in these verses?

- Those who don't work have no sense.
- Those who don't work hard (are slack in their work) are closely associated with those who destroy things.

These are some really, really strong things to say against those who don't work hard. Laziness is not a good thing.

How might we fall into a pattern of being lazy?
To be a good worker, how important is it to see work that needs to be done and to do it without being asked?
Can you give me examples of work that you might do—even without being asked—at home and other places?

Listen to this Scripture:

Whatever you do, work at it with all your heart, as working for the Lord, not for human masters, since you know that you will receive an inheritance from the Lord as a reward. It is the Lord Christ you are serving. (Col. 3:23–24)

When we are working, or when there is work to be done—no matter what that work is—who are we supposed to think of as our boss?

How hard should we work for a boss who loves us and has made huge sacrifices for us?

Summing It Up

You worked hard rolling that bucket around, but there was a nice little treat afterward. And there are often rewards in life when we fight the tendency to be lazy and instead work hard. In fact, the Bible even says that those who refuse to work shouldn't just be given food.

> For even when we were with you, we gave you this rule: "The one who is unwilling to work shall not eat." (2 Thess. 3:10)

Many, many people don't work hard in this world. It can be very easy to get lazy. We want to develop a good work ethic. There are times we should work hard, without complaining about it. If we do, we'll stand out in a good way.

It helps if we remember that God is really our boss, and he deserves our very best efforts. And there are many types of rewards that follow hard work.

Sometimes it may seem that nobody even notices the hard work you do. But the truth is, if you develop the habit of working hard and doing good work, it will not go unnoticed.

> Do you see someone skilled in their work?
> They will serve before kings;
> they will not serve before officials of low rank.
> (Prov. 22:29)

Another translation ends the verse this way: "he will not stand before obscure men" (ESV).

We may not serve a king like some countries in the world do, but we serve the King of Kings, right? He doesn't miss a thing. So let's not be lazy but rather, when there is work to do, let's work hard, do a good job, and do it with all our heart!

Magnetic Christians

THEME: Strong magnets are made to cling tight—but they also repel. As Christians, we're to cling to some things and repel others—and not get the two mixed up.

THINGS YOU'LL NEED

- [ ] *Ring magnets*, which are donut-shaped and often have a ceramic coating. A quick online search will give you plenty of options. I saw a set of six at HomeScienceTools.com for under $10.
- [ ] *Anything metal* to test the magnets with
- [ ] Optional: if you pick up a wooden dowel or a length of PVC that would fit nicely in the "donut" hole of the magnetic ring, that would be great. Cut the rod down to about 12 inches. If you're doing this, it would be even nicer to have the rod drilled into a block of wood as a base so it can stand upright all by itself.

Advance Prep

Test two of the ring magnets. As you put them together one way, they should cling together nicely. Now flip one of the ring magnets and try to put them together. They should repel each other.

If you made a stand as mentioned in the optional bullet point above, slide one of the ring magnets onto the rod. Now add another ring magnet—but flipped to repel the other. As you slide it down the rod, the two magnets will fight each other, and instead of clinging together, the second magnet should hover above the other in midair.

Do this with the rest of the magnets, alternating each one as you slide it down the rod so that all of the magnets are hovering on the rod. You can even tap the magnets. They'll bounce but won't cling to each other. Nice job . . . you're all set!

Now, there is one more thing to do in advance. Make a list of things Christians should avoid and another of things we should cling to. Put Bible verses with them if you can. You can enlist friends to help, if you'd like. If the kids have trouble coming up with ideas of things they should cling to or repel as Christians when you do this activity with the family, pull out your list.

Running the Activity

1. If you made the stand, slide the magnets onto the rod so that they cling together nicely as one big stack. Now pull the magnets apart and start over.
2. Have the kids take turns putting the magnets on the rod—but this time be sure that every other ring magnet is flipped so that they repel each other. You should have the entire stack of them hovering on the rod—none of them clinging to each other.

If you didn't make the little rod stand, give each of the kids a pair of ring magnets and ask them to put them together. Once that's done, have them flip one magnet the other way and try to put them together again. They should find it impossible to keep them together.

Teaching the Lesson

We all know that good, strong magnets are designed to cling tight to another magnet when you put them together—or when you put them up to metal. (If you have some metal objects to attach to, it would be great to demo that at this time.)

But sometimes we forget the other quality that magnets possess. The power to repel.

Strong Christians should function a lot like strong magnets—with the ability both to cling and to repel. The important thing is to know *what* to cling to and what to repel.

> What are some things we're to cling to—things we're to hold tightly to?
>
> What are some things we're to repel—things we're to avoid?

There are plenty of good things we should cling to. *If you made a list yourself, this would be a great time to reference it.*

- **Good character.** Being a person of integrity means being honest and dependable and doing the right things—even when nobody is looking (Prov. 10:9).
- **Wisdom and a good reputation.** These are more valuable than treasure . . . definitely something to hold on to (8:11; 22:1).
- **Love and faithfulness.** Proverbs 3:3–4 makes it clear we're to never let go of these.

- **Instruction.** This includes the good things you've been taught by parents or mentors (4:13).
- **A good attitude.** It's easy to lose this . . . so we must hold on to it tightly (Phil. 2:14–16).
- **Truth.** We're to lock on to the truth of God's Word (Prov. 23:23).

The list could go on and on, but ultimately there is one thing—or one person—we need to cling tightly to.

Fear the LORD your God and serve him. Hold fast to him and take your oaths in his name. He is the one you praise; he is your God, who performed for you those great and awesome wonders you saw with your own eyes. (Deut. 10:20–21)

> My soul clings to you;
> your right hand upholds me. (Ps. 63:8 ESV)

How do we cling to the Lord?

There are also things we're to repel as Christians, things we're to avoid. Here's a short list.

- **Hypocrisy.** Jesus reminded us to avoid the hypocrisy that characterized the religious leaders of his day (Matt. 6:1–6, 16–18).
- **Arguing.** It's important to avoid fighting and arguing (Prov. 20:3).
- **Sexual immorality.** It's God's will that we stay pure (1 Thess. 4:3).
- **Coarse joking and unwholesome talk.** We're not to have anything to do with it, as in totally distancing ourselves (Eph. 4:29; Prov. 4:24).

- **Bad friendships.** The Bible tells us why to avoid these: they will corrupt us (1 Cor. 15:33).
- **Pride.** To have a healthy fear and respect of God, we're actually to hate pride—that's strong language (Prov. 8:13)!
- **Lying.** This is something God hates, which is a good reason to avoid it (6:16–17).

How do we repel the things we're to avoid? *See what the kids say about this, but some little reminders would be to surrender to the Holy Spirit, stay in the Word to be reminded of what to aim for and what to avoid, and with God's help put the Word into practice.*

Summing It Up

Ring magnets give us a picture of how we're to react when it comes to good things and evil things in this world. As Christians, we want to be like magnets. We want to cling tightly to some things and consistently repel or avoid others. The Bible encourages us to cling to God and avoid evil.

> The highway of the upright avoids evil;
>> those who guard their ways preserve their lives.
>>> (Prov. 16:17)

Love must be sincere. Hate [or avoid] what is evil; cling to what is good. (Rom. 12:9)

The secret to whether a ring magnet will repel or cling has to do with the direction it's facing. Let's make sure we're facing the right way so that we avoid the evil things we should stay away from and cling to the good things we're to hold tightly to.

Remember No More

THEME: The completeness of God's forgiveness and the gratitude we should feel as a result.

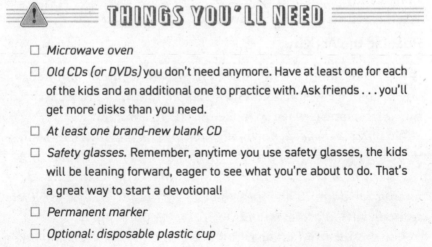

THINGS YOU'LL NEED

☐ *Microwave oven*

☐ *Old CDs (or DVDs)* you don't need anymore. Have at least one for each of the kids and an additional one to practice with. Ask friends . . . you'll get more disks than you need.

☐ *At least one brand-new blank CD*

☐ *Safety glasses.* Remember, anytime you use safety glasses, the kids will be leaning forward, eager to see what you're about to do. That's a great way to start a devotional!

☐ *Permanent marker*

☐ *Optional: disposable plastic cup*

Advance Prep

You'll definitely need to practice this ahead of time when the kids aren't around.

1. Put on a pair of safety glasses.
2. Place the plastic cup upside down in the microwave, dead center.
3. Set a CD on top of the cup.
4. Set the microwave timer for 6–8 seconds . . . that's all you need.
5. Start the microwave.

I've probably microwaved hundreds of CDs—and I can tell you that your family will love it. The microwave handles it just fine too. The CD will make some interesting zapping and popping noises—but it's all pretty harmless stuff. It looks great, though, so you'll hold the family's attention while you do your little demo. When you do this with the kids, douse or dim the room lights for a more dramatic view.

Running the Activity

A CD holds about 700 MB of memory. We could fit hundreds of novels on one CD and access any chapter, line, or word we wanted. But what happens when we nuke the CD in a microwave?

Go through the sequence of steps outlined in the Advance Prep section. You may want to dim or turn off the lights for better viewing.

After the microwave turns off, flip on the lights and open the microwave door. Remember, the CD is going to be hot for a few seconds, so don't touch it until you can handle it safely.

Look at the front and back of the CD. How does it compare to a new CD? Look at the spiderwebbing on the CD. The CD we just microwaved can never be played again.

And this little demo illustrates a truth about life that I'd like to talk with you about.

Teaching the Lesson

We talked about the CD capturing tons of memory. Did you know there's a record being kept of each one of us? God doesn't miss anything.

- He sees what we've done—good or bad.
- He knows our thoughts—good or bad.
- He hears every word we say—good or bad.

In fact, the Bible says we'll have to give an account for everything we say, do, and think.

> Nothing in all creation is hidden from God's sight. Everything is uncovered and laid bare before the eyes of him to whom we must give account. (Heb. 4:13)

And that brings us back to the biggest problem of life.

- Since everybody sins—and God doesn't miss anything—all of us are guilty of sin (Rom. 3:23).
- God is just—and he must punish sin.
- The Bible says the wages of sin is death (6:23).

We are in an impossible situation.

But God, in his great, great love for us, didn't leave us in that hopeless position. He provided a way of escape for us . . . a rescue from our sin. And that way is Jesus.

- The Bible tells us that when Jesus died on the cross and was raised to life again, he paid the penalty for our sin.
- When we come to him, confessing our sins and believing he alone can save us, God forgives us. It is like the CD that can no longer be played after being in the microwave. God will choose to remember our sins no more.

> I, even I, am he who blots out
>> your transgressions, for my own sake,
>> and remembers your sins no more. (Isa. 43:25)

What a fantastic truth! And one that should fill us with gratitude. Once we have been forgiven of our sins, God will never play them back again. He will never dig them up and expect us to pay the penalty for them somehow. Our sins are gone. What a wonderful God we serve!

> The LORD is compassionate and gracious,
>> slow to anger, abounding in love.
> He will not always accuse,
>> nor will he harbor his anger forever;
> he does not treat us as our sins deserve
>> or repay us according to our iniquities.
> For as high as the heavens are above the earth,
>> so great is his love for those who fear him;
> as far as the east is from the west,
>> so far has he removed our transgressions from us. (Ps.
>> 103:8–12)

If we claim to be without sin, we deceive ourselves and the truth is not in us. If we confess our sins, he is faithful and just and will forgive us our sins and purify us from all unrighteousness. (1 John 1:8–9)

Summing It Up

While God never misses one sin we commit, he has provided a way for the penalty of every one of our sins to be paid for in full—through Jesus, God's Son. This should be a motivating factor in our lives. If somebody rescued you and saved your life somehow, wouldn't you be really, really appreciative? Well, that's what Jesus did for us. He's our rescuer. The gratitude we feel for what he has done for us should drive us to live more grateful and obedient lives.

Let's each take a blank CD and write our name and date on it with a marker. Now write the words MY SIN in bold letters on the CD. If you have surrendered your life to God, confessing your sin and trusting that Jesus paid the price in full, your record of sin will not be played back to you. It will not be remembered by God. That's a truth I hope you'll never forget. And to help us remember, we'll each have a turn to microwave our CD. Then I want you to keep it somewhere in your room. Every time you see that microwaved CD in the future, remember the wonderful thing God did for you through Jesus.

A Special Word for Parents

Keep some blank CDs on hand. If one of the kids really messes up at some point in the future, and they ask your forgiveness but are still feeling bad about what they've done, even after you've forgiven them—pull out a blank CD. Write their name and the date on it and nuke it in the microwave. Hand it back to them as a powerful demonstration of what true forgiveness is all about.

As you give them the ruined CD, reassure them that you have forgiven them—and that you'll never play it back. And then, of course, you'll need to remember not to bring up whatever it was that they did wrong. You've got this!

Fix a Flat

THEME: Being stuck on the side of the road is not a good thing
. . . and it can happen to us figuratively as Christians.
The important thing is to get back on the road—and fast!

THINGS YOU'LL NEED

☐ *Access to a car . . . along with the jack assembly and the owner's manual where it explains how to change a tire.*

☐ *A flat, safe place to change a tire.* For some, that may be your driveway. If that isn't a possibility, and you have to do it on the street, consider going to a nice, quiet corner of a parking lot instead so you can be away from any potential traffic.

Advance Prep

If you've never changed a tire, you may want to practice it once before getting the kids involved. Maybe ask a friend who's done it before to come over and show you the ropes. Better yet, invite your experienced friend over when you plan to do the devotional with the kids—and ask them to help change the tire. After they're done, you can follow up with the application time.

One more little prep thing. Go online and pull up a clip of a pit crew changing tires. Check NASCAR. It's amazing how fast a car can get back in the race when the pit crew has practiced. Keep that clip handy . . . it would be great to use it when you sum up the lesson.

Running the Activity

Get the kids together and go through the procedure for changing a tire step-by-step. You're not just talking them through it. For more impact, you actually want to change the tire.

And remember, if this makes you at all uncomfortable, explain this activity to a friend who has experience changing a tire. See if they'll come over to help teach the kids how to change a tire. Honestly? A lot of guys in particular would jump at the chance to be the expert and have your kids as an audience.

1. Be sure to have the owner's manual out to show your kids how you're following the procedures. And if your friend is changing the tire and feels they don't need the manual, ask them to follow it anyway. It will be important when teaching the kids the lesson.
2. Before you start changing the tire, be sure to go over any safety guidelines needed based on the ages of your kids.
3. Let the kids help where appropriate for their age and safety, such as loosening the lug nuts and pumping the jack to lift the car.
4. Rather than actually putting the spare on—which would mean you'd have to jack it back up and put the original tire back on

later—just take off the good tire and put it right back on again as if it were the spare.

Once the tire is back on with the lug nuts tightened, the car is lowered, and the tools are put away . . . you're ready to teach the lesson.

Teaching the Lesson

What are some things a person needs in order to change a tire?

How important was it that we had the instructions for changing the tire?

What are some of the most common causes of a flat tire?

If we were actually out driving on the highway and got a flat, what are some of the dangers of fixing that flat there on the side of the road?

If you were pulled over in a dangerous, high-traffic place, how important would it be to fix that flat—fast—so you could get back on the road?

A handful of questions like these above will get the kids thinking, setting things up perfectly to transition into a spiritual truth.

Sometimes as Christians we can be cruising along the highway of life and suddenly we get a flat . . . something that keeps us from moving forward.

What kind of dangers might Christians face if they find themselves stuck and not moving forward?

Do Christians have a manual—a guidebook—that takes them through the steps to fix what is holding them back?

How might a wise, experienced friend be able to help?

How important is it to be able to fix the problem quickly and get back on the road?

There are all kinds of things that can slow us or stop us as Christians, "nails" that flatten our tires. What are some things that can keep us from moving forward?

- Fear and worry are very real nails.
- Busyness can work like a nail, keeping us from following God as we should.
- Screen time is often a big fat nail that slows us in doing anything of eternal good.
- Sin can work like a nail, stopping us from moving forward with Jesus.
- A tragedy, a loss, bad news, something hurtful said to us . . . all these things and more can put us on the side of the road.

Some of these things just happen in life—and there is nothing we can do to keep them from happening. What we *can* do is practice going to the Word, the Bible, and following its instructions to get back on the road. As we practice, we'll get better and better at it . . . so the little nails of life won't stop us for long. The quicker we can get back on the road, the less chance we'll have of getting hurt some other way.

Summing It Up

Imagine if we were on a highway, and a truck a quarter mile ahead of us dropped a huge box of nails on the road. We wouldn't drive through the nail minefield. We'd go around it. Take an exit. Find another way or pull over so we didn't get a flat.

In a similar way, we want to do all we can to avoid the nails in life—the things that can slow us down or flatten all forward progress.

Let's do that in the Christian life too, and avoid the nails as best as we can. And when something does slow or stop us, we can learn to deal with that quickly so we aren't in danger long. The longer we stay on the side of the road, the greater our chance of getting hit—of being delayed further in another way.

- We need to practice trusting God, so when we pick up a nail of fear, we know how to deal with it, and it doesn't leave us helpless on the side of the road.
- We need to practice obeying Scripture and avoiding temptation. Then we'll know how to dodge the nails . . . the sin that can sideline us. Even if we do mess up, we'll know how to "change that tire" and get back on the road fast.

We want to work at putting the Word into practice, so even if we do end up on the side of the road, we'll know what to do and won't be there long.

But everyone who hears these words of mine and does not put them into practice is like a foolish man. (Matt. 7:26)

To wrap things up, show the kids the clip of a pit crew in action. It's amazing to see how fast and efficient the crew is—but that only comes with practice. Remember, the more we work at putting the Word into practice, the less time we'll spend on the side of the road.

Pin the Tail on the Donkey— with a Twist

THEME: If we're going to become the people God wants us to be, we need to listen to the right voices.

THINGS YOU'LL NEED

- ☐ *Pin the Tail on the Donkey game.* You don't actually need an official Pin the Tail on the Donkey game, but if you have one—or pick one up at a party store—that's great. Otherwise, use anything you can tape on the wall, even a piece of paper.
- ☐ *Tail with tape on it.* If you are just taping a piece of paper to the wall, you'll need to make a "tail" and put a piece of tape on that.
- ☐ *Blindfold, scarf*, anything to cover the eyes of your volunteer
- ☐ *A couple of "whacky noodles,"* those flexible floating toys kids play with in pools. You can find these in many stores like Walmart and Target in season. You can also find them in pool supply stores. Pillows could be

substituted for whacky noodles, but realize pillows can pack more of a wallop than you'd like your blindfolded person to receive.

☐ *The more people involved in this devotional, the better.* You can probably run this just fine with three people, but it will be a bit more effective and fun with more. Consider rounding up some volunteers. Maybe your kids can invite a couple of friends, or a grandparent, aunt, or uncle can join.

Advance Prep

Once you've picked up the list of supplies, you're all set. No other advance prep is needed.

Running the Activity

1. Have your donkey poster or target attached to the wall, and explain to the kids that a blindfolded volunteer needs to take the "tail" and pin it to the poster. Tell them there will be a couple of important things that make this game a little different from usual.

2. Two others, armed with whacky noodles, will be the "distracters." Their goal is to keep the blindfolded one from attaching that tail anywhere near the target. While not allowed to touch or push the blindfolded volunteer, they can hit them with the foam noodles—and give bogus verbal instructions—to keep the volunteer off course.

3. Now, explain to your blindfolded son or daughter that *you* will give the right instructions. If they focus on your voice and do what you say, you'll lead them to the target.

4. So get your volunteer blindfolded, turn them around a couple of times, and send them off for the target. The distracters will try to confuse them, but you must continually give them good, solid instructions so they can reach the target.

Once you've done this with one of the kids, you may want to rotate to give the kids the chance to play different roles.

Teaching the Lesson

How hard was it to get the tail to the target with the distractions of the whacky noodles? How hard was it to get the tail to the target with all the bogus instructions going on? How much did the distracters enjoy keeping the blindfolded one off course?

This is so much like life. Ephesians 2:10 says this:

For we are God's handiwork, created in Christ Jesus to do good works, which God prepared in advance for us to do.

- There are things God has planned for us to do.
- There is a person he has planned for each of us to become.

But there are many distractions—and distracters—in this world. Things and people who keep us from hitting the plans God has for us. Can you think of any?

However, there was one more voice in this little game we played. The voice of your [mom or dad, or whoever else is leading this], who encouraged you and tried to show you the right direction. That is a picture of one of the roles of parents. Anybody want to guess what it is?

Fathers, do not exasperate your children; instead, bring them up in the training and instruction of the Lord. (Eph. 6:4)

One of a believing parent's deepest desires is that their kids grow to be solid Christians, follow the Lord, and put the Word into practice. That they'd have wisdom and integrity and make wise, biblical choices. That is not often the same deep desire your friends may have for you. Can anybody tell me what I mean by that or give me an example?

While we don't get it right all the time as parents, certainly our desire for you is always for the best. You can trust my voice. I won't deliberately lead you wrong. That isn't the case with everyone. Some people are more like distracters, keeping us from hitting the mark as to the kind of people we should be.

Summing It Up

Life is full of voices telling you what to do and where to go. Often, as they do, they keep insisting they're giving you good information, even if they aren't. We, your parents, have been given a job by God to protect you, provide for you, and prepare you for your future. The older you get, the more "other" voices will influence you . . . or not. The choice is yours. I pray you'll choose to listen to the right voices in your life. You'll be so much better off.

Car Wash

THEME: Rules can be annoying, but they're in place to prevent trouble and damage that would result if they weren't followed.

THINGS YOU'LL NEED

☐ *A good automatic car wash*, the type you drive into—and stay in your car as it is washed

Advance Prep

Locate the car wash and check out their options. Do they offer wax, or anything else that might do more to protect the car over the long run other than the wash itself? Plan to get the wash with the extra options when you bring the family.

Running the Activity

1. Take the family to the car wash. Get them as engaged as possible when you're choosing your options. Tell them you really want the car to look good and be protected. Maybe call out the options. "Should we get the underbody flush option? Should we get the wax option?"

2. Now, when you line the car up to go into the car wash itself, you'll see the warning sign. Read it aloud to the kids. "The sign says to roll up all the windows, put the car in neutral, and keep my foot off the brake. What do you think . . . should we do it?"

3. The age and personality of your kids will totally influence their answers. But you may want to mess with them a little. "You sure we should follow their rules? How about I just keep one window down?" Now actually roll down the window by one of your kids—or by your spouse if they're in the car. Don't roll down your own window. If they protest a bit, that's perfect. Even as you move forward . . . just before the water hits . . . tease one or two of them with a quick partial roll-down of their window.

If you get some screams, I have to say congratulations. That is pure gold. You'll really be driving the point of this lesson home.

After you leave the car wash, it's up to you if you want to vacuum the inside and so on. It isn't part of the lesson, but you'll have lots of hands to help do the job. Your call on that.

As soon as you leave the car wash, you'll want to go somewhere to tie in the spiritual truth of this lesson. I like taking the kids for a snack at some fast-food place. You'll have a captive audience, and the food naturally helps them listen better.

Teaching the Lesson

There was a warning sign just before we went into the car wash that listed some rules. Anybody remember what some of those rules were?

Now, can you tell me why they had those rules? What would have happened if I didn't follow them?

Would you agree that the rules were about protecting us and our car? How crazy would it have been if I said something like this just before we went into the car wash?

- "Hey, I paid good money for the car wash—and it's my car. I should be able to decide if I want to keep my windows down and get the inside of our car soaked and coated with wax."
- "I don't think I'll keep the car in neutral like it says. I'll put the car in reverse. Would that honestly mess up the transmission? Or maybe I'll put it in park. I doubt that will cause any damage to the car."

That kind of attitude would be crazy, right?

Sometimes we have that same I-don't-see-why-I-have-to-follow-the-rules attitude when it comes to the things we're told to do—or to avoid—in the Bible. We may be okay with following some "rules," but others? We don't see the point.

The point of the rules in the Bible is generally all about our protection. Failing to follow the Bible leads to damage, hurt, pain, loss, and regret. Disobedience is costly on every level. Often in this life . . . and definitely in the one to come. Obeying or disobeying is often a life-or-death issue.

> The highway of the upright avoids evil;
>   those who guard their ways preserve their lives. (Prov. 16:17)

Following the Word is all about our protection. And many, many, many good things are in store for those who surrender to Jesus and follow him in obedience. Just look at the fruit of the Spirit—the love, joy, peace, and so much more that come when we are walking with the Lord.

> Do not be deceived: God cannot be mocked. A man reaps what he sows. Whoever sows to please their flesh, from the flesh will reap destruction; whoever sows to please the Spirit, from the Spirit will reap eternal life. (Gal. 6:7–8)

The above passage is just one of many reminders in the Bible that failing to follow the Word always ends badly.

Summing It Up

Sometimes we fool ourselves. We say we love Jesus or sing worship songs to him, but we really aren't being careful to follow the commands and warnings in his Word. Do you know what God says about that?

We know that we have come to know him if we keep his commands. Whoever says, "I know him," but does not do what he commands is a liar, and the truth is not in that person. But if anyone obeys his word, love for God is truly made complete in them. This is how we know we are in him: Whoever claims to live in him must live as Jesus did. (1 John 2:3–6)

Yes, there are rules in the Bible. Commands. But they're not there to make life miserable. They're there because God loves us. They're about our protection. They're there so we can become the kind of people God designed us to be and so we can do the things he's planned for us to do.

All Scripture is God-breathed and is useful for teaching, rebuking, correcting and training in righteousness, so that the servant of God may be thoroughly equipped for every good work. (2 Tim. 3:16–17)

We followed the warnings at the car wash—and our car is better off for it. We are too. Following the rules kept us from getting wet. Let's look at God's warnings and commands the same way.

> The decrees of the LORD are firm,
>   and all of them are righteous.
> They are more precious than gold,
>   than much pure gold;
> they are sweeter than honey,
>   than honey from the honeycomb.
> By them your servant is warned;
>   in keeping them there is great reward. (Ps. 19:9–11)

Christians and Flameproof Balloons

THEME: Christians should be different in many ways from those who don't have Christ, especially in the ways they react when the heat is on.

 ═══ **THINGS YOU'LL NEED** ═══

☐ *12-inch balloons.* Buy the good teardrop-shaped ones at a party store or online, which are often described as "helium quality." They're a little thicker or better quality—and consequently not as likely to break. Don't settle for the cheaper dollar-store balloons. They're likely just going to disappoint. And don't even think about the little balloons made for water-balloon fights, which are just too thin to do the job.

☐ *Access to a sink, hose, or even a couple of water bottles* so you can fill the balloons halfway with water

☐ *Candle in holder.* A candle set in a holder that allows you to get close to the flame is best. If the candle is in a jar, you won't be able to get the balloon close enough.

Advance Prep

Once you've picked up the supplies, you're all set. It will only take you a couple minutes to test this, and I really encourage you to run through this before doing it with the kids.

Running the Activity

1. Fill a balloon with water until it grows to approximately the size of a large grapefruit. You can fill it at the sink, or if you're planning to be outside or away from the house when doing it with the kids, use the hose or a water bottle or two. Tie a knot in the end of the balloon.
2. Dry the balloon off so no drips of water are on its outside.
3. Fill another balloon with air. Inflate it to be about the same size as the water-filled one. Tie a knot in the end.
4. Take the activity outside if possible. If you choose to do it inside, be sure there is nothing in the area that may catch fire. When I did this, I put the candle in the sink. There was nothing nearby that could burn, and if I needed some water, all I had to do was turn the faucet on.
5. Light the candle.
6. Have one of the kids hold the air-filled balloon by its knot. Now have them move the balloon right into the flame. It should pop immediately.

7. Now have one of the kids hold the water-filled balloon the same way and move it into the flame for a few seconds—and then back out. The balloon didn't pop!

8. Repeat the above step, letting the kids take turns doing it. You're showing them over and over that the water-filled balloon is reacting completely differently than the air-filled balloon.

9. Now have one of the kids hold the balloon over the candle for an extended time. The tension will mount as they expect the balloon to pop at any moment. I've held the water-filled balloon over the flame for as much as a minute at a time. The bottom will blacken, but the balloon should hold. That's another advantage of doing this in the sink. If the balloon does burst, the mess will be in the sink, not on the table or the floor.

Teaching the Lesson

Let's imagine that all people are balloons. Those who don't have Christ are air-filled ones. Those who do have Christ are balloons with water inside.

Christians should be different from the world in many ways. Especially when we are in tough situations—when the heat is on. What do I mean by that?

- When we're tired.
- When we're hungry.
- When things aren't going our way.
- When we're afraid.
- When someone is giving us a hard time.
- When we really mess up somehow.

The list could go on.

The balloon that was full of hot air burst. And we see that in real life, don't we? Some people blow up when things are hard or are not going their way. They get angry or have a meltdown. Some of that is to be expected from people who don't have Jesus.

But it should be different for Christians. We have Jesus inside us, not just hot air. Just like the water inside the balloon kept it from bursting, we have the Living Water inside us with the ability to keep us cool and calm—even when the heat is on.

But how do we do that? How do we keep from falling apart when things are tough? What do you think?

Trusting God is certainly a big part of it. You can trust him to guide you as you rely on him more and more.

> Trust in the LORD with all your heart
>> and lean not on your own understanding;
> in all your ways submit to him,
>> and he will make your paths straight. (Prov. 3:5–6)

Knowing he loves us and wants us to bring our cares to him is part of it too, don't you think?

> Cast your cares on the LORD
>> and he will sustain you;
> he will never let
>> the righteous be shaken. (Ps. 55:22)

And I think another key element to keep us from falling apart when the heat is on is what the apostle Paul speaks of: a reliance on Jesus for strength we don't have.

I know what it is to be in need, and I know what it is to have plenty. I have learned the secret of being content in any and every situation, whether well fed or hungry, whether living in plenty or in want. I can do all this through him who gives me strength. (Phil. 4:12–13)

Summing It Up

Because we have the Living Water residing in us, we should react differently to hardships in life than people who don't have Jesus. Or let's put it this way: we have the *capability* to react differently. And we will act differently as

- We trust God to direct us.
- We bring our cares, worries, fears, and frustrations to him, knowing he cares for us.
- We learn the secret to being able to handle anything: going to Jesus for strength.

Then, more and more we'll be like that water-filled balloon . . . able to hold together when others simply fall apart. That's what I want, don't you?

Three-Legged Race

THEME: The importance of dating only another solid Christian.

THINGS YOU'LL NEED

- ☐ *Scarf* to tie legs together
- ☐ *Stopwatch or stopwatch app on phone*

A Special Word for Parents

Think your kids are too young for this? Maybe. But this is one of those truths that has real advantages if taught young, well before they're of dating age. That way, when the dating years come, they've already known for a long time what God desires for them in this area. And when the kids do get to an appropriate age for going on a date, the idea of only considering a Christian to date won't come as a surprise—or prompt an argument.

Advance Prep

The only advance work you'll need is to find a good place to run a three-legged race/obstacle course. The best course may simply be "Run to this spot, go around that object, then go around the next object, and then run back here." Remember, they'll be tied together, so stairs can be fun but also really dangerous.

Running the Activity

1. Have the kids pair up and stand side by side, so close that they're touching. Now tie their inside legs together. Wrap the scarf around their ankles and maybe up to their shins. You want their legs to be securely together, like they're a complete unit. There's less chance of anyone twisting an ankle that way.

2. Explain the route they're to take, time them as they run the course, and jot their results down. If you have more kids, you may want to ensure that all of them get a turn, but that isn't essential.

3. After they've run the course with both runners facing forward, have them team up again just as they did the first time—but with a twist. This time, you'll have one of the runners face forward and the other backward. Tie their legs together as before, and have them run the course while you keep track of their time.

The amount of time it takes when one is facing backward should be significantly longer. Congrats. You're all set to teach maybe the strongest lesson you can about the need to date only another Christian.

Teaching the Lesson

Start by comparing their course times facing the same direction versus facing opposite directions.

Can anyone share how much more difficult the race became when they were facing opposite directions?

Imagine a company runs a three-legged marathon race over rough terrain where anybody who crosses the finish line within a set time wins a million dollars. How would you want to run that race: with both of you facing forward, or with one of you facing backward? Can you imagine anyone risking such a huge prize by running that three-legged race with one partner facing backward?

There is another race many people will run at some point in life. It's like a three-legged race in some ways, because it's run with two people. And it isn't just a 26.2-mile marathon. It's a race that will last years and years. I'm talking about *marriage*.

Marriage is two people joined together as one for the rest of their lives.

What kind of rough terrain might they face in their marriage?

How might marriage be harder if the husband and wife aren't facing the same direction? If their views about life and God and heaven and hell are different from each other?

What if their views about raising kids, forgiving others, giving money to the church, or attending church are different from each other?

What other perspectives might be different if one person in a marriage is a Christian and the other is not?

If a person is a true follower of Christ, they know that Jesus is their Lord. They know they must live the way Jesus teaches. They can't just live how they feel.

How might it be valuable in a marriage when both husband and wife realize that they can't just do whatever they feel like doing but rather answer to God for how they treat each other? How might that make a marriage better or stronger?

Check out this passage from the Bible.

> Do not be yoked together with unbelievers. For what do righteousness and wickedness have in common? Or what fellowship can light have with darkness? What harmony is there between Christ and Belial? Or what does a believer have in common with an unbeliever? (2 Cor. 6:14–15)

The Bible is clear that we want to avoid marrying someone who is not a solid Christian. And if we're not to marry them, it surely makes sense not to even start dating them.

One of the most important differences between a believer and an unbeliever is that the believer has the Holy Spirit and a "new nature," but the unbeliever doesn't. How might that impact a relationship?

Here's another verse that is critically important to understanding why a relationship with an unbeliever is dangerous—and will end up being so much less than ideal.

> For the flesh desires what is contrary to the Spirit, and the Spirit what is contrary to the flesh. They are in conflict with each other, so that you are not to do whatever you want. (Gal. 5:17)

- This verse reminds us that even though that non-Christian you may really want to date is a nice, nice person . . . eventually there will be problems. Conflicts. Fights. Because you're going to change in ways the other person can't.
- As Christians, we have the Holy Spirit giving us new desires and perspectives. And these desires and perspectives will be

very different from those of somebody who doesn't have the Holy Spirit.

So even if we seem to be very similar in a million ways with that non-Christian . . . it can't stay that way. Because the Holy Spirit will be changing our heart, and we'll soon be on different pages. We'll be growing apart, and there are only two ways to grow back together.

1. The unbeliever becomes a believer.
2. The believer walks away from their faith.

In the case of the first, we can't bank on the person we date becoming a believer, right? And in the case of the second, the idea of walking away from God is unthinkable, isn't it?

Which brings us back to the point of not even dating an unbeliever. The risks are too great.

What about "missionary dating," which is dating someone with the purpose or hope or expectation that they'll become a genuine believer?

- It's a risk . . . and a big one. Solomon, despite being very wise, married women who were not believers in the one true God, and eventually they caused him to compromise massively in his faith and lead an entire nation astray.
- The point is, dating an unbeliever is more likely to change the believer than the other way around.

Summing It Up

When is the best time to make a decision about being committed to only dating a solid believer: before you date them or after you've gone on a few dates?

Think about when you were tied for that three-legged race. Were you any closer physically when both of you faced forward than when one of you faced the opposite way?

- No . . . your legs were still touching no matter which way you faced.
- And that can be the danger of dating an unbeliever. You may feel just as close to them as you would a believer, but according to the Bible it won't stay that way. The Spirit wants to give you new desires—which will be in a different direction than an unbeliever will want to go.

Marriage can be a great thing, and any believer can have a million-dollar one. But you want to be sure the person you marry is as firmly committed to the Lord as you are. If not, like running that obstacle course with one of you facing the opposite way, you're going to be facing hardships and conflicts and slowdowns. Those will keep you from the million-dollar marriage you could've had if you'd married a believer who was fully committed to following Christ and the principles the Bible teaches us to live by.

Stick This in Your Head

THEME: This one is a wild card as far as the theme goes. You can teach just about anything with this object lesson. We'll go with "loving God and loving others" for this one, but you can adapt this to teach a wide range of topics.

 ## THINGS YOU'LL NEED

- ☐ *Chemical-resistant gloves* for the person doing the demo
- ☐ *Safety glasses* for you and all who will be observing
- ☐ *Styrofoam strips.* You can buy sheets of Styrofoam insulation at the hardware store that are about 1 inch thick and 2 feet wide. Cut four 2-inch strips out of the sheet of Styrofoam using a saw or a utility knife. That will give you one test strip and three to use with the devotional.
- ☐ *Wide-mouth jar.* A rinsed-out pickle jar works nicely. You'll be feeding the styro-strips into the jar, so you want its mouth to be 2 inches wide or close to it.
- ☐ *Acetone.* You can pick this up in the hardware store, usually in the paint-supply area. You won't need much, so if you can buy a quart

rather than a gallon, that will be plenty. *Note: We'll also use acetone for Activity 24, Time Gobblers.*

☐ *Cutting board or piece of plywood* about the size of a placemat, or a 9 × 13 glass baking pan works great. In case any acetone spills, the wood or pan will protect your table underneath.

☐ *Permanent marker*

☐ *Clean paper plate*

☐ *Tape*

Advance Prep

1. Draw a face on the paper plate and tape it to the side of the empty pickle jar. The jar will enable the plate to stand up on end.

2. Take one of the Styrofoam strips and write LOVE GOD in big letters along the length of it. Write LOVE OTHERS on the second strip and SONGS, STORIES, ETC. along the third strip.

3. Wearing gloves and safety glasses, pour about two inches of acetone into the pickle jar. Be sure you don't fill the jar more than halfway.

4. Feed the blank test Styrofoam strip into the solution so you get a feel for how fast it dissolves. You don't want to insert the

You can teach other principles with this object lesson instead of the ones I chose here. Write those things on the strips instead. Anything you want the kids to remember works really well. I'd limit the lesson to two or three principles at most, though, or else your devotional time will go too long and you'll lose their attention.

strips too slowly, so the object lesson goes too long, and you don't want to go so fast that the acetone can't keep up.

5. Put the cap on the acetone until you're ready to have your teaching time with the kids.

Running the Activity

Arrange the paper plate with its face toward the kids. The glass jar it is taped to should be hidden behind the plate so only you see it. Be sure to take the cap off the jar so that you're ready. Have the strips labeled LOVE GOD and LOVE OTHERS off to the side. You only want the one labeled SONGS, STORIES, ETC. visible right now.

Brainstorm with the kids the fact that sometimes things get stuck in our heads. Part of a song. Scene from a movie or book.

Let's imagine the face on this paper plate is you. These songs or whatever can get stuck in your head. Whatever it is, you can't seem to get it out of your head. It can keep looping and looping in your brain—even when you don't want it to.

Let's demonstrate what that's like.

With safety glasses and gloves on, take the Styrofoam strip with the words SONGS, STORIES, ETC. and feed it right into the acetone in the jar. From the angle the kids are at, it looks like you're sticking the strip into the paper plate head. Keep pushing that strip into the solution until it is completely gone.

Yes, songs, stories, comments, all sorts of things can get stuck in our heads—even when we don't want them to. We just can't seem to get them out of our heads. And often the stuff that gets stuck isn't even important. We tend to forget the important stuff we should remember and remember the silly stuff we'd like to forget.

Teaching the Lesson

Once Jesus was asked what the most important command in the Bible was. When he answered, he even added a bonus by giving them number two on the list.

> One of the teachers of the law came and heard them debating. Noticing that Jesus had given them a good answer, he asked him, "Of all the commandments, which is the most important?"
>
> "The most important one," answered Jesus, "is this: 'Hear, O Israel: The Lord our God, the Lord is one. Love the Lord your God with all your heart and with all your soul and with all your mind and with all your strength.' The second is this: 'Love your neighbor as yourself.' There is no commandment greater than these." (Mark 12:28–31)

What are some examples of how we should be loving God? What would that look like?

What are some examples of how we should be loving others?

Why do we fail to do these types of things more often?

Could it be that often we get so busy or so focused on ourselves that we just forget how much God wants us to love him and love others?

Wouldn't it be great if every time we were about to choose how to spend our time, we asked ourselves how well our decision would show love for God—and let that answer help us make our choice?

Wouldn't it be great if every time we were about to say something nasty to someone else or do something mean, we remembered how important Jesus said it is to love others?

How can we do a better job of remembering to love God and love others?

Summing It Up

When Jesus prioritized all the commands in the Bible and came up with the two most important ones, he definitely wanted people to remember them.

What do you think? Are these the types of things we'd like to get stuck in our heads?

Let's do that. *Pull out the last two Styrofoam strips and feed them into the jar.*

I'm praying that we remember these important commands more often than we currently do. And by doing this visual demonstration, I hope you are prompted to remember God's two greatest commands whenever you have decisions to make—and whenever you're tempted to ignore someone else or treat them rudely.

Love God. Love others. Let's pray right now that God makes these stick in our heads! *Close in prayer.*

Time Gobblers

THEME: The need to guard against things in our lives that gobble up way more time than they should.

 ═══ **THINGS YOU'LL NEED** ═══

- ☐ *Chemical-resistant gloves* for the person doing the demo
- ☐ *Safety glasses* for you and all who will be observing
- ☐ *Styrofoam packing peanuts,* the type that come in a box to keep something fragile from breaking. If you have some from a shipment you received, great. Otherwise, ask around! Or you can get them in most office supply stores or mail outlets like UPS, FedEx, and so forth. You'll want at least enough to fill a 3-gallon pail.
- ☐ *Soup cans.* Just two of the regular 10- or 11-ounce cans are perfect. Rinse them well.
- ☐ *Acetone.* You can pick this up in the hardware store, usually in the paint supply area. You won't need much, so if you can buy a quart rather than a gallon, that will be plenty. *Note: We'll also use acetone for Activity 23, Stick This in Your Head.*

☐ *Cutting board or piece of plywood* about the size of a placemat, or a 9 × 13 glass baking pan works great. In case any acetone spills, the wood or pan will protect your table underneath.

Advance Prep

1. With gloves and safety glasses on, pour an inch or two of acetone into a clean soup can. Remember, acetone is a solvent, so don't do this on the kitchen table without a cutting board or pan underneath. If you spill the solvent on a nicely finished wood surface, the finish won't be so nice afterward.

2. Now take the Styrofoam peanuts and drop them in the soup can with the acetone. They should dissolve quickly. Keep adding the peanuts until you're pretty confident about how this all works.

3. Take the can with the solvent outside, away from the house. The acetone will evaporate, and the residue for the Styrofoam will solidify. Now it is safe to toss the can in the garbage.

Running the Activity

Add the acetone to the soup can before the kids get there. Have the Styrofoam peanuts piled up on the table. Ask the kids to take a seat, put on safety glasses, and make a pile of the peanuts in front of them with as many pieces they feel will fit inside the soup can without stuffing them in.

Now start putting Styrofoam into the can—just like you practiced earlier. Ideally, you won't let them see that there is a solution inside. But even if they do, no big deal. Once you've finished off the pile that one child built, start adding the peanuts from the next pile. You will probably get all of them to fit in the can as they melt in the solvent.

Okay, you're ready to move on to a spiritual truth for the kids.

Teaching the Lesson

Wasn't it absolutely surprising how many more of the peanuts fit into the soup can than you thought? As you've probably figured out, there was a solution in the can. A solvent that dissolves Styrofoam. Actually, it's the same ingredient used in nail polish remover. Good thing your fingernails aren't made of Styrofoam!

In life, there are things that tend to gobble up our time just like the acetone dissolved the Styrofoam.

There are some things that take time and are absolutely needed. Can you name some?

- Sleep, homework, and eating all take up chunks of time, but they're needed.

There are other things that take up pockets of our time that aren't absolutely necessary. Can you think of any?

- How about the time we spend texting or tracking with friends somehow online?
- How about the time we spend on video games?
- How about how much time we spend on sports?

It's not that any of these things are wrong or bad, but it's easy to spend too much time in one of these areas. Would you agree with that?

Be very careful, then, how you live—not as unwise but as wise, making the most of every opportunity, because the days are evil. Therefore do not be foolish, but understand what the Lord's will is. (Eph. 5:15–17)

We need to make the most of our time. We need to be wise. Someday we'll have to answer for how we spend the time God has given us. That's kind of a scary thought!

Summing It Up

The solution gobbled up a lot more of the peanuts than we probably thought it would.

- How might that be happening with the amount of time we spend texting, gaming, or whatever? Could we be spending more time at it than we think?
- If we are finding opportunities to text or play video games but not finding the time to spend in the Word or with God on any given day, does that sound out of balance to you?
- What can we do to limit the amount of time our phones gobble up?
- How can we put some of that time toward a better use—toward something that would count for eternity?

A Special Word for Parents

As parents we need to be asking ourselves the same questions. How are we using our time wisely—or unwisely? We may need to confess this to our spouse and our kids, and have a little talk with God about it as well.

Clean Up Your Act

THINGS YOU'LL NEED

- ☐ *Garden hose*
- ☐ *Towels*
- ☐ *Supplies to wash the car*

Advance Prep

You can actually do any number of activities with this one. I'm suggesting washing the car. It is fairly quick and easy. And you'll have the hose right there when you need it. Feel free to swap this activity out with a different one. The point we're making has to do with complaining or arguing when given a task to do.

Running the Activity

1. Have all your supplies ready to wash the car: bucket, sponge, hose, soap, towels. Have the kids wear clothes that you won't mind getting wet. Now explain for family devotions they're going to help you wash the car—but there'll be a little twist with this project.

2. Anyone complaining or arguing in any way about the job, what they're told to do, and so forth will be sent for a "Clean Up Your Act penalty." This CUYA station is nothing more than a garden hose. If one of the kids complains or argues, you'll march them to the designated spot and give them a shot from the hose. It's up to you if you want to explain in advance what will happen if they complain—or if you'll wait until someone messes up. Personally, I'd wait.

3. Now, wash the car with the kids, and be sure to assign each one tasks to do. Keep your ear out for any complaining. Any arguing. Is your spouse there with you? If so, be sure they keep their ears open too.

4. When somebody messes up, and you're going to give them a quick rinse, back up a safe distance so the water pressure isn't too forceful. I'd also have them turn their back so you don't risk hitting them in the face—or anywhere else that may hurt.

5. Now give them a shot from the hose. They'll be shocked, and their siblings will love it. Once they've been doused, you'll send them back to their car washing duties—and keep an ear out for arguing or complaining. If they complain about being hosed down, they just earned another rinse cycle.

I imagine some of the kids will snitch on the others, claiming to hear a complaint or insisting their brother or sister was arguing. Do your best to play judge—or hose them both. Have fun with this!

One word of caution. You may want to be the only one carrying out the CUYA penalty. If a sibling does it, you may find there will be shots to the face or other areas that would hurt, and tempers may flare. Not a good idea.

Once the car is done—and hopefully there has been some extra rinse activity—you're ready to transition into a spiritual truth.

Teaching the Lesson

When I sent any of you to the CUYA station, you really had no say in the matter, right?

- There was no trial.
- There was no jury.
- I alone decided whether you were guilty or not . . . and I carried out your sentence.

There may have been some reasons you complained or argued that you believe were valid. Like you had a right to complain or argue. So maybe it didn't seem fair that I shot you with the hose anyway.

Listen to these verses from the Bible.

Do everything without grumbling or arguing, so that you may become blameless and pure, "children of God without fault in a warped and crooked generation." Then you will shine among them like stars in the sky as you hold firmly to the word of life. And then I will be able to boast on the day of Christ that I did not run or labor in vain. (Phil. 2:14–16)

The Bible tells us to do things without grumbling. Without complaining. Without whining. And without arguing.

That isn't always easy, especially when we're tired, hungry, scared, proud, insecure—or when things just don't seem fair. But God wants us to work on this.

How might your life be better if you didn't argue or complain?
How might family life be better if you didn't argue or complain?
How might things be better if I did less arguing or complaining?

Let that last one sink in a bit.

A Special Word for Parents

Here's something to think about. If you'll be vulnerable enough to ask yourself, *How might things be better if I did less arguing or complaining?*—and make changes where needed—you'll hit a critical crossroads with family devotions. The end result? Your kids will respect you more. And if they do, they'll listen to you more. Sound good? Definitely. Also remember the flip side. If you fail to ask the question or fail to change your ways, you will have taught the kids a dangerous lesson. They'll see you as a hypocrite, unwilling to live by the standards the Bible lays out. This is serious stuff.

Summing It Up

When we talk about doing things without arguing or complaining, it doesn't mean we can't question things or see if there are other options we'd like better. But the key is often how we do that. We can ask questions or offer creative alternatives without complaining or arguing.

Doing what the Bible says generally isn't easy. Remember, God doesn't want us to keep trying to "measure up" so that we're good enough for him. Rather he wants us to see that we can't live this Christian life on our own. He wants us to reach out to him and give him permission to change us—our hearts—to be more like Jesus.

Let's do that, starting with the issue of arguing and complaining. Let's go the rest of the day without doing it, okay?

A Special Word for Parents

If they buy into the challenge of going a day without arguing or complaining, encourage them along the way. If they do well on day 1, keep adding days. Set small goals for them to reach for. "Let's not argue or complain for another day, okay?"

And no matter how they do, be sure you, as the parent, are putting this into practice yourself. Not just with the kids but as you relate to your spouse too. You can change the whole family climate in such good ways by doing exactly that.

Last point I'll make on this is for you, the parent. Remember, you're an example to the kids, so watch how you talk to and about others. The complaining thing also goes for your job. And also the way you talk about work or the boss when you're at home. Not that you can't express your disagreement with management's decisions, but do it in a respectful way that isn't complaining. Speak the truth in love.

Rubber-Boned Christians

THEME: It's important to have strong "spiritual bones" so we can stand firm as Christians. We need to avoid things that tend to weaken our spiritual bones—and immerse ourselves in things that strengthen them.

THINGS YOU'LL NEED

- ☐ *Chicken bones.* Drumstick or thigh bones work great.
- ☐ *Glass jar with cap*, big enough for the bone to stand upright in and be covered with liquid. A small pickle, jam, or olive jar works great.
- ☐ *Vinegar.* Get a whole bottle of regular white vinegar. You'll need enough to fill the jar, and there are other devotions in this book where vinegar is needed.
- ☐ *Safety glasses.* Nobody wants vinegar in their eyes, right?

Note: You're going to use the same object lesson here as in Activity 27, The Acid Effect of Envy, but each will have an entirely different application. So as you're collecting supplies, realize you'll need all these same things again.

Advance Prep

Ideally, try this out ahead of time if you haven't done The Acid Effect of Envy devotional yet. You'll go into the devotional with more confidence if you've seen firsthand just how vinegar will weaken chicken bones.

It will take several days for the experiment to do what it needs to do, so keep that in mind when you're scheduling family devotional time.

Running the Activity

Have a chicken dinner with the kids at least three or four full days before you want to do the actual lesson with them.

1. Ask the kids to save some of the drumstick and thigh bones. In fact, ask them to help you clean all the meat off them.
2. When the bones are all thoroughly cleaned, pull out the glass jar and put some of the bones inside. Keep at least one of the bones on the side to use as a comparison later.
3. Add vinegar to the jar so that the bones are completely submerged. Twist on the jar lid.
4. Explain that you're going to leave the bones in the vinegar until you have family devotions in a few days.

Teaching the Lesson

After the bones have been soaking in the vinegar for a full three or four days, you're ready to go.

1. *Have the kids put on safety glasses and pour the vinegar from the bone jar down the kitchen drain. Have them rinse the bones with water and dry them off.*

2. *Pass the bones around. Compare the ones you had in the vin-egar to the cleaned bone you simply kept on the side from your chicken dinner.*

Bones need calcium to keep them rigid. Because we left the bones in the vinegar for days, and because vinegar is an acid, it dissolved the calcium in the bones. That's why the bones are so weak now. That poor chicken wouldn't be standing very well if it had bones like this!

As Christians, we are told to stand tall and strong in various ways.

Be on your guard; stand firm in the faith; be courageous; be strong. Do everything in love. (1 Cor. 16:13–14)

What does it mean to stand firm in the faith? There's a lot to it, but can you give me an idea?

If we want to stand strong, how important is it to actually know and understand what we believe as Christians?

The chicken bones became weak by being immersed in an acid that slowly dissolved their strength. What kinds of things might we surround ourselves with that can weaken our faith if we stay immersed in them?

How might friends weaken our faith or our resolve to stand strong?

How might the amount of time we spend online be like being im-mersed in bone-weakening acid—especially if we aren't spend-ing time in the strengthening Word?

The changes that took place in the chicken bones didn't hap-pen overnight. The weakening of the bones was slow. So slow that it wasn't something we actually noticed happening. We didn't see any evidence that the bones were getting weaker and weaker and weaker—until the damage was done. The bones looked okay on the outside, even though they were really getting weaker.

> How is that basic fact similar to how we can get weakened in our faith without even realizing it's happening?

> With this in mind, are there any practices you need to change or habits you need to break so that your faith doesn't get weakened?

> Are there some things you need to spend less time with because they're keeping you from spending the time you need in the Bible to strengthen yourself in the faith?

Those verses we looked at in 1 Corinthians 16 reminded us to be courageous and strong. How do we need courage and strength when it comes to changing some of our faith-weakening practices?

Summing It Up

Rubber-boned chickens can't go very far. And Christians with rubber-boned faith won't go far either.

> If you do not stand firm in your faith,
> you will not stand at all. (Isa. 7:9)

God has a journey for us. Places to go. Things to do. A person to become. And we're going to need good, strong "faith bones" to do that. Let's work on getting the weakening acids out of our lives, okay?

The Acid Effect of Envy

THEME: The need to guard against envy—not just because it's wrong but also because it will weaken us.

THINGS YOU'LL NEED

You're going to use this same object lesson here as in Activity 26, Rubber-Boned Christians, but each will have an entirely different application. Flip back to that lesson for the list of Things You'll Need, as well as for the Advance Prep and the Running the Activity instructions.

Advance Prep

See note above.

Running the Activity

See note above.

Teaching the Lesson

Have the chicken bones been in the vinegar for a full three or four days? Okay, you're ready to go.

1. *Have the kids put on safety glasses and pour the vinegar from the bone jar down the kitchen drain. Have them rinse the bones with water and dry them off.*
2. *Pass the bones around for comparison. The ones you had in the vinegar—and the cleaned bone you simply kept on the side.*

What do you notice about the bones that sat in the vinegar for several days versus those that didn't?

Does anybody know why the bones are so weak now . . . almost rubbery? Vinegar is a mild acid. But if you give vinegar enough time, it's still strong enough to dissolve the calcium in chicken bones. And bones need calcium to keep them rigid.

This weak, almost-rubber chicken bone illustrates an important truth of the Christian life. Did you know that there is something we can "soak" in that will weaken us in very real ways?

> A heart at peace gives life to the body,
>   but envy rots the bones. (Prov. 14:30)

The Bible says here that *envy* can weaken us as if we had rotten bones. That doesn't sound good.

How might being jealous or envious of others weaken us?

How might being jealous or envious of friends weaken our relationship with them?

There are a million things we can be envious or jealous of. Can you name any?

Sometimes we can be envious of other Christians and the good things they have. Looks. Abilities. Friends. Family. Opportunities. Proverbs 14:30, the verse we read a few moments ago, contrasts peace with envy. When we are jealous or envious, we cease to have peace . . . and that's not a good place to be.

Anger can be a really bad thing, but the Bible describes jealousy as being potentially worse in its ability to destroy.

> Anger is cruel and fury overwhelming,
>> but who can stand before jealousy? (Prov. 27:4)

Envy and jealousy are wrong. How do we get away from this emotional acid that can eat at us?

As with any sin, we need to realize we are doing wrong. We need to confess. And we need to ask God to help create a right attitude in us. Also, the more time we spend in the Word, the more our perspective will be balanced, and the more we'll be able to distance ourselves from the acid of envy.

Sometimes we can get jealous and envious of non-Christians or other Christians who don't seem to even try living the way the Bible teaches. They may appear to have a great life. It may even seem like they don't have many problems.

King David struggled with that kind of frustration at times too. Psalm 37 has a great perspective that can help us when we're feeling envious of people who aren't Christians . . . or those who aren't living like a Christian should.

> Do not fret because of those who are evil
>> or be envious of those who do wrong;
> for like the grass they will soon wither,
>> like green plants they will soon die away. (vv. 1–2)

Be still before the LORD
>> and wait patiently for him;
do not fret when people succeed in their ways,
>> when they carry out their wicked schemes.
Refrain from anger and turn from wrath;
>> do not fret—it leads only to evil.
For those who are evil will be destroyed,
>> but those who hope in the LORD will inherit the land. (vv.
>>> 7–9)

Better the little that the righteous have
>> than the wealth of many wicked;
for the power of the wicked will be broken,
>> but the LORD upholds the righteous. (vv. 16–17)

These verses help us see things with an eternal point of view. Do you see how having the right perspective about others is important if we are to shed envy? What are some of those right ways of thinking that we need to focus on?

Summing It Up

If we had just dipped the bones in the vinegar and then rinsed them off instead of letting them soak, do you think they would have gotten weak like they did?

Definitely not. We all have moments where we get a flash of jealousy or envy. We need to confess that and go to the Word to get a change of perspective. And we need to do that quickly. Stewing in the acid of envy will hurt us, weaken us, and definitely reduce our ability to stand strong as Christians.

In the Bible, Paul lived with contentment, which helped keep him from getting jealous or envious. He trusted God with whatever situation he was in.

I am not saying this because I am in need, for I have learned to be content whatever the circumstances. I know what it is to be in need, and I know what it is to have plenty. I have learned the secret of being content in any and every situation, whether well fed or hungry, whether living in plenty or in want. I can do all this through him who gives me strength. (Phil. 4:11–13)

Paul learned to rely on God for his true needs and to trust him in whatever situation he was in. He knew God could help him handle anything that came his way. That led to peace and contentment. And it led to a strength Paul wouldn't have had if he'd been stewing in the juices of envy and jealousy.

Let's work at doing the same, okay?

Will It Sink or Swim?

THEME: When facing anxiety, kids often feel they're alone—and that no one really understands their situation. God cares about their concerns, even if they seem small to others. God can help us in ways we'd never, ever expect.

THINGS YOU'LL NEED

- ☐ *Large plastic bin or garbage can,* anything you can fill with water. You'll want something big enough to accommodate various items that you'll "test" with the kids to see if they float or sink.
- ☐ *Basketball,* or any type of rubber ball that floats
- ☐ *Bowling ball weighing 8 pounds or less.* The weight is important. We need this bowling ball to float.
- ☐ *Ax head.* You can find a replacement ax head at hardware stores.
- ☐ *Handful of coins*

Advance Prep

Finding the lightweight bowling ball may be the biggest challenge for this devotional. Here are two suggestions that haven't failed me yet.

1. Post on social media that you're looking to borrow a bowling ball (remember, 8 pounds or less) from someone local.
2. Call local bowling alleys and ask if you can borrow a ball for a couple of days.

Don't make finding the right plastic garbage can/bin harder than it needs to be. All you need is something you can fill with water. If the container is big enough to hold a basketball and deep enough to allow heavier items to sink, it will likely work fine. You could do this demo in the bathroom tub or kitchen sink if needed. You can do it in a pool. Going bigger often makes the lesson that much more fun and memorable for the kids.

The ax head. Depending on where you live, a neighbor or friend at church is likely to have an ax with a split handle in their garage, like I do right now. Ask if you can borrow the ax with the understanding that you'll be removing the split handle. You'll be doing them a favor—and helping them stay safe! And borrowing gives you a chance to explain what you'll be teaching your kids, which helps you be a faithful witness in a small way.

Running the Activity

You have the container filled with water and the basketball, bowling ball, ax head, and coins lined up alongside it. Now take each item, one at a time, and hold it up. Each time, ask the kids the same question: "When I put this in the water, will it sink or float?" After getting their response, drop the item in the water.

1. Start with an obvious one—the ax head.
2. Then do the basketball.
3. Then do the handful of coins.
4. Save the bowling ball for last.

They should be surprised that the bowling ball floats. Perfect! Now you're ready to tie in a nugget of spiritual truth.

Teaching the Lesson

None of you were shocked when the ax head dropped straight to the bottom, right? There's an interesting story in the Old Testament about an ax head that sunk—but only at first. Then a crazy thing happened that defied all the laws of nature.

Let's look at the story in 2 Kings 6:1–7.

- A man was cutting trees along the Jordan River. As he took a swing, the ax head flew off the handle, splashed into the river, and disappeared to the bottom.

- The man who lost the ax head was alarmed. The ax had been borrowed—and now there was no way he could return it.

Honestly, it's only an ax head. But the text says the man "cried out." He was really, really concerned about this. He was anxious. He had no idea what to do. He likely felt it was an impossible situation that couldn't be fixed.

There are times in life when we'll feel just like the man who lost the ax head. Anxious. Worried. We'll feel we're in an impossible situation that can't be fixed.

And often, there will be people around us who may seem to think our situation is not that big of a deal. Our situation may seem unimportant to others, but it really matters to us. We'll feel alone. We'll feel nobody understands us.

Have you ever felt that way?

Did any of you expect the bowling ball to float?

No, likely you didn't foresee that, any more than the man expected his ax head would float.

But there is an important principle here that we'll want to remember. Anybody know what that might be?

God can do the absolutely unexpected. He can defy all laws of nature if he chooses to. He can bring solutions that we can't imagine.

Summing It Up

The man who lost the ax head did something critically important when he was overwhelmed with anxious thoughts. What was it?

- He cried out in his distress. He talked to someone about what was bothering him, what was making him fearful and anxious.
- If the man had kept his situation quiet, if he'd held it in, his situation wouldn't have changed.
- He made his situation known to Elisha, a man of God.

When we're feeling anxious, keeping it to ourselves may guarantee our situation doesn't change.

- I want you to know you can bring anything to me. Helping you through tough situations is part of my job.
- I also want you to know you can bring anything to _____. (Mom, Dad, fill in the blank here. A grandparent. A youth pastor/leader. A solid follower of Christ who is close to your family or involved in the life of any of your kids.)
- And remember to bring all your anxious thoughts to God. Sometimes he chooses to do the absolutely unexpected . . . like the day he made the ax head float. Often, he works out a solution that we would've never predicted.

How happy do you think the man in the Bible story was that he didn't hide his anxious feelings?

One more thing . . . and this is really, really important. In the Bible account, the lost ax head may seem like a small thing to you. Honestly, it may have seemed like no big deal to the man's friends at the time too. But it was a big deal to the man who lost it. God cared enough about that man to help him—even with something that may have seemed like a small thing to others.

Always remember that God cares enough about you to help with whatever you're feeling anxious about, even if others don't seem to understand.

Cast all your anxiety on him because he cares for you. (1 Pet. 5:7)

God has said,

> "Never will I leave you;
>   never will I forsake you."

So we say with confidence,

> "The Lord is my helper; I will not be afraid." (Heb. 13:5–6)

The Bible doesn't guarantee God will "fix" your situation like you may hope he will, but the Bible says he cares. You won't be alone. Sometimes he'll do the impossible for us, but he'll *always* be with us as we go through whatever is creating our anxiety, no matter what.

And even if our situation doesn't seem to change, God promises to give us something that is nothing short of an absolute miracle: peace for our anxious mind. Wow, what a great reason to bring our anxiety to God! Check out this passage of Scripture. It is definitely worth memorizing.

Rejoice in the Lord always. I will say it again: Rejoice! Let your gentleness be evident to all. The Lord is near. Do not be anxious about anything, but in every situation, by prayer and petition, with thanksgiving, present your requests to God. And the peace of God, which transcends all understanding, will guard your hearts and your minds in Christ Jesus. (Phil. 4:4–7)

I See That Hand

THEME: There are plenty of people who like the idea of being a Christian, but they aren't exactly "raising their hands," eager to be disciples of Jesus. Could it be that they're missing something?

THINGS YOU'LL NEED

- [ ] *Nitrile or latex surgical-type disposable gloves*, available in most pharmacies and in the paint department of most hardware stores. The powder-free variety works perfectly.
- [ ] *Duct tape*
- [ ] *Clear drinking glasses*, at least two, but it would be nice to have a glass for each of the kids.
- [ ] *Vinegar*
- [ ] *Baking soda*
- [ ] *Measuring spoons*, both tablespoon and teaspoon
- [ ] *Permanent marker*. Optional, but fun.

Advance Prep

You'll definitely need to test this in advance. The activity is quick and easy, but you'll do it better and smoother with the kids if you've practiced it beforehand.

1. Slip the open end of a glove over the mouth of a clear glass. A tight fit is what you're looking for. If the fit is too loose, find a different glass with a wider mouth, perhaps from the dollar store, or check the mugs you have in the house.
2. Now, remove the glove from the glass.
3. Pour 3 tablespoons of vinegar into the glass.
4. Pour 2 teaspoons of baking soda into the glove and shake it down inside so the powder is in the fingertips.
5. Without letting the baking soda slip out of the glove and into the vinegar, wrap the open end of the glove over the mouth of the glass as you did before, ensuring a tight seal. If you need to use duct tape to make the seal tighter, this is the time to do that. The glove should be hanging limp over the side of the glass.
6. Lift the fingertips to quickly shake the powder into the vinegar, and then let go. The glove should sag back down at first, but as the baking soda mixes with the acidic vinegar, carbon dioxide is formed. That will fill the glove and make it stand up tall, like it is at attention, until the reaction slows and the carbon dioxide escapes.

Fun stuff, right? You're ready to do this with the kids! What about the optional permanent marker? That's to draw scars and veins on the glove. If you're like me, you'll probably turn it into a creepy, monster-like hand.

Running the Activity

1. Have the baking soda in the fingers of *your* glove, and put the glove on your glass of vinegar, before the kids are present.
2. Now bring the family into the room where you have a glass for each of them ready and waiting. You may want the vinegar measured and poured into each one—or have them help you do it. Your call.
3. Invite the kids to slide a glove over the mouth of their glass so that it looks like yours. Help them with this step if needed.

Explain that you want to see if their hand will raise. Tell them it may need a little nudge from them, so invite them to lift the fingers of the glove up and shake it a bit. Obviously, that won't make a bit of difference—because there is no baking soda in their gloves . . . only in yours. Their gloves should fall limp and lifeless to the side of the glass again.

Say, "Let me show you what I mean." Now raise your glove for a moment to let the baking soda drop into the glass. Then release it and stand back.

The kids will be amazed! And they'll know you're messing with them somehow. Now is your chance to explain that two ingredients are needed to make the hand raise—but they only had one. They only had the vinegar.

Now pull out the baking soda, add 2 teaspoons to each glove, and let them try the experiment again. This time every "hand" in the room should go up.

Teaching the Lesson

Let's imagine that the vinegar represents becoming a Christian and the glove represents our willingness to actually be a disciple.

Now, a true Christian is saved. They have the Holy Spirit. But they aren't always so quick to "raise their hand" and be counted as a disciple. And we see that evidenced by their lives.

True or false: Being a disciple means we actually follow Jesus. That we see him as our leader—and we are not just willing to follow him and obey him but actually do so.

True or false. I'll mention some things we can do. Say "True" if it is something Jesus expects his disciples, his followers, to do. Say "False" if it isn't.

- Tell our non-Christian friends about Jesus—how he loves them and died for them.
- Encourage our believing friends to obey Jesus with the decisions they make.
- When we feel God wants us to do or say something, we are quick to do it.
- We love others—even the ones who are hard to love.
- We treat others nicely—unless they aren't nice to us. Then we give them a real dose of "an eye for an eye" type of treatment.
- We're sure to give ourselves plenty of "me" time to mess around on the computer or whatever.
- If we're only kids, God doesn't expect us to spend time reading the Bible on our own or praying.

Why is it we can be so slow to obey what Jesus teaches, or to raise our hand and be counted as one who is truly working at being a disciple of Jesus?

If we aren't quick to "raise our hands," to obey Jesus and do the things he expects of true disciples, could it be that we're missing a key ingredient—like you were missing the baking soda at first?

I'm going to read some verses; see if you can find the two ingredients needed to be a disciple. These are the ingredients that truly drive our desire to obey and follow closely. Listen for the first ingredient in this passage.

> We love because he first loved us. Whoever claims to love God yet hates a brother or sister is a liar. For whoever does not love their brother and sister, whom they have seen, cannot love God, whom they have not seen. And he has given us this command: Anyone who loves God must also love their brother and sister. (1 John 4:19–21)

Do you see it here? The first key ingredient for being a disciple is *love for God*. Not just a mushy "I love Jesus" type of thing but real love for God—which will be evidenced by living like Jesus did and by loving others.

The second ingredient is something the woman who anointed Jesus's feet with expensive perfume had in Luke 7:36–50. Let's pull out our Bibles and read this passage together.

This woman definitely had the first ingredient. She loved God. And here she is displaying great gratitude for what Jesus did for her. There's the second key ingredient. *Gratitude*.

Summing It Up

If we find ourselves slow to "raise our hands" to say "Yes, I want to be a true disciple of Jesus," chances are we are lacking love for God and gratitude for what he did for us through Jesus.

The more we think about and realize what he did to save us—and how undeserving we are of the great mercy he shows us—the more we'll love God. The more grateful we'll be. And this love for God and gratitude for what Jesus did for us will be used by the Holy Spirit to nudge us to do the things that disciples do.

I pray that all of you are raising your hands inside your hearts right now. That you'll be filled with love for God and with gratitude. And that you'll live that out as a disciple of Jesus by following and obeying him!

Wrong Place, Wrong Time

THEME: If we don't keep our Christian batteries charged, we'll likely end up in some dangerous situations!

THINGS YOU'LL NEED

☐ *Your mobile phone*—completely uncharged

☐ *A remote place to take the kids*

☐ *Phone charger*, the type you can use in the car

Advance Prep

Running your phone down until it's out of juice is the big thing here. You don't just want your battery low as you teach this lesson . . . you'll want it to be completely dead.

Find a remote place to bring the family. Someplace you'd definitely feel more comfortable if you had your phone. Depending on where you live and the time of year, you can probably come up with a couple of great ideas. Stay creative.

You'll be tempted to just "talk" the kids through a scenario with this lesson. "Imagine my phone is dead and we're in the middle of a desert." Shortcuts like this are easier to pull off, but they are way less memorable and effective. Put in the effort. It's always worth it.

Running the Activity

You've taken the kids to the remote place. For the purposes of this lesson, I'll imagine you've gone somewhere out in the country a bit. Away from civilization. But remember, you can bring the kids anywhere that could potentially be a bit risky or dangerous under different circumstances.

Look around. Use your imagination. How might being in this spot become risky—or even dangerous—if we were here at the wrong time or if our situation was a little different?

What if our car was broken down here in some way. How might it get dangerous?

What if we were here in the middle of the night. How might it get dangerous?

What could show up (animal or enemy) that might make our situation more dangerous?

What is one thing that might make even a scary or dangerous situation much safer? *Hold up your phone to steer their thoughts.* A phone could change everything. I'm not really alone when I have my phone. I can instantly connect with someone who can help, right?

What if I told you I didn't bother charging my phone before coming here? How smart would that be?

Now is the time to show them that the phone isn't charged. And you're all set to teach the main point of the lesson. Whether you do it in the remote spot you've chosen or drive them someplace else is totally up to you.

Teaching the Lesson

In our world, we hate to go anywhere without a mobile phone. It keeps us connected to our world and keeps us safe in many ways.

How is this similar to our need as Christians to stay connected to God?

How do we stay connected to God and "charged" as Christians?

Reading our Bible daily and praying may sound a little cliché, but it's still the right answer. So how can you make that more real for your kids?

We can be very dedicated to keeping our phone charged—which only keeps us connected with our world.

Why are we so likely to be less disciplined when it comes to keeping our connection charged with God—the Creator of the universe?

How might we put ourselves in danger because we've failed to stay connected to God?

I took you someplace today that I'd normally not go without a working phone. Sometimes, even as Christians, we go someplace we shouldn't—*because* we're not connected very well. Can you think of any examples of that?

- We may be on a website we shouldn't be on.
- We may be with friends who are doing things we shouldn't be doing.
- We may be at some event that we really don't belong at as a Christian.
- We might be watching a movie, listening to music, or reading a book that we know is not appropriate for us as Christians.
- We might be on a text thread that we shouldn't be on because of where the conversation is going.

Failure to stay fully charged in our relationship with the Lord can lead to all kinds of dangers . . . physical, spiritual, and emotional. It's my hope that we all work at staying connected to the Lord.

It's important, and according to this verse below, it can be a life-or-death issue. Certainly, it can mean *spiritual* life or death.

> The highway of the upright avoids evil;
> those who guard their ways preserve their lives.
> (Prov. 16:17)

Summing It Up

This would be the time to make a point of plugging your phone into the charger you have in the car.

It's reckless to drive to a remote place with a dead phone. And once we realize our phone isn't charged, how foolish would it be to stall on recharging it?

If you've been a little hit-and-miss with charging your Christian batteries with God, I hope you'll get on that right away. How will you start doing that today?

A Special Word for Parents

Mom and Dad, this would be a great time to help the kids lay out a plan to be more disciplined with regularly charging their batteries with God. You may want to tell them what works for you. If you're not in the habit of charging your spiritual batteries as often as your mobile phone battery . . . maybe talk to the kids about how you're going to do things differently too.

Who Floats Your Boat?

THEME: The friends you choose and confide in are important. They'll help keep your head above water . . . or not.

 THINGS YOU'LL NEED

☐ *Access to a canoe.* Do you live close to a camp? Ask around at church or on social media. When they understand what you're doing, likely you'll find someone who will let you borrow their canoe. They may even offer to help!

☐ *Two paddles*

☐ *Coast Guard–approved life jackets* for all those in the canoe—and those on the dock if applicable

☐ *Small bucket* for one of the passengers in the canoe

☐ *Two adults.* For safety reasons, you'll want one adult in the canoe and one on shore.

Advance Prep

Well in advance of leading this devotional, read the story of Amnon and his friend and adviser, Jonadab, in 2 Samuel 13. You'll want this story to sink in a bit. Note how bad of a friend Jonadab is to Amnon at two very distinct times in the chapter.

The details of the story are pretty mature, so you'll want to give more or less detail depending on the age of your kids. I'll keep it pretty basic in the Teaching the Lesson section below—but I don't avoid the sordid parts. Honestly, your kids can probably handle more than you think. And the importance of the lesson is often best illustrated by telling the whole story without sugarcoating the uncomfortable parts. I've seen this happen so much where kids are taught only partial truths in Sunday school: they grow up thinking they know familiar Bible stories, but sometimes key information was left out . . . and they're missing important details God included in the Bible for probably a number of reasons, including their protection.

One more thing to think about: Jonadab was a horrible influence on Amnon. And the text tells us that Jonadab was Amnon's cousin. You've probably lived long enough to see that there are members of your extended family who are dangerous, right? Remember, you are the protector of your kids. You'll want to be very honest when talking with them about this. There may even be a family example you'd give—or a warning to be on their guard around "Uncle Harry" or one of their cousins.

Remember, this is about protecting your kids from bad influences. Don't skip this lesson, saying maybe you'll teach it when they're older. Do you have any kids that can't handle this? Maybe let them sit on the sidelines for this lesson and teach it just to the older ones.

Now, if some of your kids are too young for this, they may not catch the sordid details anyway, so no worries. But your older ones need this truth. Kids ages eight to ten need to be aware there are people (including relatives) who give bad advice or have predatory tendencies. This lesson opens the door to some really good and needed discussion about a critical topic.

All that to say, I'd rather risk telling kids when they're too young than leaving them unprotected until they are older.

Running the Activity

1. Ideally, you'll have one person paddling in the front and one paddling in the back, and a passenger in the middle.

2. Have a destination in mind for the crew, such as "Paddle to that buoy/pier/beach and back." When selecting a destination, use your safety sense. Sometimes it's safer to have them paddle parallel to shore, so they're always in shallower water, than to choose a destination in deeper water.

3. Give them a time limit, keeping it as short as reasonably possible.

4. Give one crew member the bucket—likely the person in the middle.

5. Make sure all who will be in the boat or on a dock/pier are wearing Coast Guard–approved life jackets.

6. Now give your crew their destination and explain that you want them to paddle the canoe there and back—without tipping. The job of the person sitting in the middle is to derail the work of the paddlers. This person will reach over the side with the bucket, doing their best to fill the boat with water.

7. Have them run the course, and let any other kids you may have watch from shore. Depending on how old the kids are and how far you had them paddle, the canoe will have more or less water in it. The person with the bucket may even cause the canoe to swamp or tip.

8. When they arrive back with the canoe, make sure everyone who was on shore gets to see how much water is inside it. You might even have them help you empty the water out of the canoe as you take it out of the water.

Teaching the Lesson

How much harder was it to get to the destination and back because of the person adding water to the canoe?

Did they tip/swamp the canoe—or would they likely have done so eventually if the course had been longer?

The one with the bucket had a very different goal from the paddlers. They weren't all going in the same direction, so to speak. Sometimes that's exactly what happens with the friends we choose.

There's a tragic story in the Bible that tells about one of the worst friends ever. King David's firstborn son was named Amnon. Amnon's friend and adviser was Jonadab—who just happened to be his cousin.

I'll give you some quick facts about what happened.

- King David had many wives and kids. This was a problem in many ways—but that's a different story.
- Amnon was one of David's sons. He was a young man who was secretly in love with his half sister Tamar. Ew, right?
- Jonadab knew something was on Amnon's mind and convinced him to reveal his secret.
- Jonadab suggested a scheme of lies and deception so Amnon could get Tamar alone.
- Following Jonadab's advice, Amnon raped Tamar even though she begged him not to.

This is an awful story, for sure. Amnon was a prince. As firstborn, likely he would have been headed for a royal position in the kingdom. But he definitely didn't keep his eye on that goal. Instead, he allowed Jonadab to pour water into his canoe. He took wicked advice and did an evil thing. And the story doesn't end there.

- Amnon never said he was sorry to Tamar, the half sister he claimed to love. In fact, he wanted nothing to do with her after he sinned against her. He treated her badly.
- Tamar's brother, Absalom (Amnon's half brother), was very, very angry with Amnon, and he began to make an evil plan of his own.
- Two years later, Absalom invited all his half brothers to a banquet—including Amnon. People probably thought Absalom had gotten over what Amnon did. But during the banquet, Absalom had Amnon murdered.

News got to King David that Absalom had killed all of David's other sons—which of course was not true. Jonadab was with David at the time, and he said this:

But Jonadab son of Shimeah, David's brother, said, "My lord should not think that they killed all the princes; only Amnon is dead. This has been Absalom's express intention ever since the day Amnon raped his sister Tamar. My lord the king should not be concerned about the report that all the king's sons are dead. Only Amnon is dead." (2 Sam. 13:32–33)

Did you catch that? Jonadab knew. He *knew*! All that time—for two years—he knew Absalom was planning to kill Amnon.

- He never warned his friend and cousin, Amnon, that Absalom intended to murder him.

- He never tried to stop Absalom from committing murder.
- He never tipped off King David so he could save his son's life.

Jonadab was about the worst friend ever. Because he was so bad,

- Tamar was raped—and her life was ruined.
- Amnon was murdered.
- King David was grieved to the core.
- Absalom eventually was killed.

This is a sad, sick story. But it is important for you to hear.

Summing It Up

Kids, we must be careful. Not everybody has your best interests in mind. Amnon learned that the hard way. He trusted Jonadab when he shouldn't have. Sometimes other people who influence you or give you advice have their own goals and plans—which can slow you down or sink you.

- These people can masquerade as your friends.
- They can even be relatives.
- These people can be a relative of one of your friends. When you are at a friend's house, you need to be careful.
- Do you know someone who would encourage you to do something that is wrong?
- Do you know someone who wants to hear your secrets, but deep down you're not sure you can trust them?

Avoid them. Talk to Mom or Dad about what you're sensing and feeling. If someone says or does something that makes you uncomfortable, talk to Mom or Dad right away. If you are at a friend's home and one of their family members is there and you feel uncomfortable, call me.

How do you think things would have gone better for Amnon if he had talked to his dad (King David) about his situation before he hurt Tamar, instead of talking only to Jonadab about it?

Just because somebody is in the same boat with you, don't assume they're paddling with you. Sometimes they have their own agenda, and it can be a dark one. Talk to Mom or Dad about what you're feeling, not just your friends, okay?

Nerves of Steel

THEME: We know we're to be strong, with faith strong enough to overcome our fears. This is easier said than done, especially when trouble is in our face—or headed there. Here's how to strengthen yourself in the Lord.

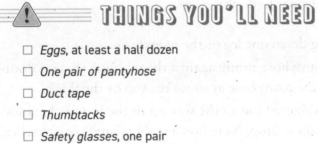

THINGS YOU'LL NEED

- ☐ *Eggs*, at least a half dozen
- ☐ *One pair of pantyhose*
- ☐ *Duct tape*
- ☐ *Thumbtacks*
- ☐ *Safety glasses*, one pair
- ☐ *Several pillows*

Advance Prep

You're going to turn regular eggs into stunt eggs. You'll basically use one leg of a pair of pantyhose as a bungee cord, while the other leg is securely attached to the molding above a door with thumbtacks (or, alternately, fastened around a tree branch).

So find a good spot to try this, then follow the steps below for a trial run before attempting this with the kids.

Running the Activity

When you actually do this with the kids, you'll have one of them volunteer to lie on the ground—directly below where the egg will drop. The pantyhose will work like a bungee cord, and you want the egg to appear as though it will hit your volunteer.

Obviously, you don't want the egg to smack their face, so you'll be doing some careful measuring beforehand. You'll need to see how far the pantyhose stretches with the weight of one or more eggs inside so you can work out how high above the ground to tie or otherwise attach the pantyhose.

You'll need a helper to do this.

1. Slide an egg down one leg of the pantyhose.
2. Hold the pantyhose firmly against the molding above a doorway. I held the pantyhose at about the top of the thigh.
3. Raise the weighted toe all the way up to the top of the doorframe, and let it drop. Note how far the pantyhose stretches. When I did this, I wasn't getting enough stretch, so I added another egg. Then another. It wasn't until I had four eggs in the foot of the pantyhose that it stretched to within 18 inches of the floor.

4. Put a stack of pillows 14–16 inches high on the floor directly below the pantyhose and do this again while a helper is watching carefully. You'll both want to make sure that the eggs won't actually touch the face of your volunteer when they're lying on the floor. As long as the eggs don't touch the pillows, you should be good. When I did this, I adjusted the pantyhose and the number of eggs so that when they dropped, they didn't get closer than 18 inches to the ground.

5. Once you're certain you have the height right, be sure the pantyhose bungee is secure and won't move. Test it one more time, okay?

Now you're ready to do this with the kids, and with a real-life volunteer in place of the stack of pillows.

1. Have your volunteer lie on the floor in place—wearing the safety glasses, of course. I'd also have the volunteer cup a hand over their nose and mouth. It will muffle their scream nicely, but the real purpose is to protect their nose and teeth in the event of a miscalculation.

2. Announce that your volunteer will need nerves of steel not to roll out of the way—but that they need to trust you.

3. When everyone is ready, raise the pantyhose leg with the egg(s) to the height you tested it at, and let it drop!

Teaching the Lesson

Sometimes it's pretty easy to have all the right Christian answers—when we're not actually in a tough situation. We know there will be times in life that will be hard or when we'll be afraid. We know the importance of trusting God in those times, don't we?

But when trouble is flying right at our face, it can be a lot harder to put all those things we know into practice. Often we want to run, hide, or scream. Or maybe we just lock up and can't seem to do anything.

In 1 Samuel 29 and 30 there is a great story about David—and what was probably the darkest hour of his life. Let me read the story to you (1 Sam. 29 and 30:1–19).

- David and his army were supposed to be joining a battle to help another king and his men.
- The king changed his mind and sent David and his men away. It was an insult, and the men were really upset about that. Now they would not bring home any plunder or treasure . . . no spoils of war.
- When the men got back to their hometown of Ziklag, they found the town had been raided by an enemy army. The wives and children of all of David's men had been taken captive.
- The men were very upset, and they blamed David. They wanted to kill him.

David was facing some massive fear. What did he do? Run for his life? Hide? No, he strengthened himself in the Lord.

But David found strength in the LORD his God. (1 Sam. 30:6)

What does it look like to strengthen yourself in the Lord?

- **It is remembering that God is in control,** he loves you, he cares about your situation, and he has promised never to leave or forsake you.
- **It is remembering the kinds of things God has done in the past,** such as in the Bible.

- **It is remembering what God has done for you** and your family or friends in the past.
- **It is remembering the truth of Philippians 4:13** and telling yourself, *I can do all things through Christ who strengthens me.*
- **It is remembering that, as followers of Christ, we are on the winning side** in the long run.
- **It is about being in the Bible**—even memorizing key verses.
- **It definitely involves talking to God,** praying to him.

Can you see how all these things would strengthen us in the Lord? These strengthen our faith—and faith enables us to stand strong.

> If you do not stand firm in your faith,
>   you will not stand at all. (Isa. 7:9)

We read over and over in the Psalms how David practiced these "strengthening" things. And when his men talked of killing him, he kicked right into his "strengthening myself in the Lord" gear.

Can you think of times when it is scary or hard to be strong—to be a faithful follower of Christ?

When friends do the wrong thing and pressure you to do the same or ridicule you if you don't?

When you bow your head to give thanks for a meal in a way that shows you hope others won't notice because you're afraid they'll make comments?

When trouble or impossibly hard things are flying right at you?

If we practice strengthening ourselves in the Lord, even when everything is going fine, how do you think we might find it becomes easier and easier to stand strong in the moments we really need to?

Summing It Up

After strengthening himself in the Lord, David led his band of men to go after the enemy army. They found them, fought them, and beat them. They rescued every last woman and child. Not a person was lost or killed. It's a fantastic story of danger and victory, and after that David's men were loyal to him for life.

Strengthen yourself in the Lord, and likely you'll be amazed at how he helps you stand strong—and do things you would have never imagined otherwise.

Be on your guard; stand firm in the faith; be courageous; be strong. (1 Cor. 16:13)

Chameleon

THEME: The company we keep matters. Sometimes the values or worldviews of our friends, or others we're around a lot, rub off on us—and stick.

THINGS YOU'LL NEED

- ☐ ¾ *cup vinegar*
- ☐ *Ceramic or plastic bowl.* You'll want to use as small of a bowl as you can to do the job.
- ☐ *1 teaspoon salt*
- ☐ *12 pennies.* Avoid the bright, shiny new ones. Clean but dull brown ones work better.
- ☐ *Plastic spoon*
- ☐ *Paper towel*
- ☐ *3 pieces of raw iron.* I used a small iron pipe fitting/connector. It was cheap and an easy find in the plumbing section of the hardware store. You just want raw iron here—no galvanized coating. Masonry

nails work well too, if they're the old iron type. Whatever you use, get three. One to test, one to do with the kids, and one in its original state so you'll have something for the kids to compare to.

Advance Prep

Test this out in advance so you can make any adjustments needed when you do it with the kids.

Running the Activity

1. Pour the vinegar into the bowl, add the salt, and stir until it dissolves.
2. Add the pennies to the bowl. Be sure they are covered by the vinegar, but don't add more vinegar than ¾ cup. We want the concentration of the vinegar/salt/copper solution to be as saturated as possible.
3. Leave the coins in the bowl for five minutes, then retrieve them with the plastic spoon, rinse them off, and set them on the paper towel.
4. Don't dump the vinegar/salt solution out.
5. Wash the iron item well and rinse it thoroughly in water. I used dish soap to be sure I removed any oily residue, which tends to be on iron fittings. I even took a wire scraper to it to be sure there was no coating on the piece, just raw iron. Now put the iron item in the bowl. Hopefully the solution will cover it, but if it doesn't, that's okay. Don't add more vinegar.
6. So far, so good.
7. Leave the iron item in the solution for thirty minutes, then take it out and set it on the paper towel to dry. You should see the

part that was in the solution now appears to be made out of copper!

Nice job! When you do this with the kids, be sure to compare the iron that came out of the solution with the piece that was never in the vinegar. The difference will be more obvious that way.

Teaching the Lesson

The piece of iron visibly changed, even as strong and solid as it was. What do you see on the part of the iron that was in the vinegar solution?

Yes, the vinegar cleaned some of the copper off the coins—and left a copper coating on the iron. This is called *plating*. It's hard to believe that pennies can have that kind of impact on iron. And there is a parallel to life here too.

Sometimes our friends have more of an influence on us than we realize. We may think we're as strong as iron and that our friends won't cause us to change. But often that isn't what happens. A chameleon changes colors to blend in with its surroundings. Often human nature is the same way. We tend to become more and more like the people we surround ourselves with.

What possible ways have friends influenced you in the past, for good or bad? Think about

- their attitude toward others.
- their attitude toward their parents.
- their values.
- their interests.
- their habits.
- their behavior.

- the way they talk.
- the way they see the world politically or in any other way.
- their attitude toward God, living out the Christian life, and so forth.
- the way they think of the opposite sex, or sexuality in general.

Can you think of someone you know or you've heard about who was influenced in good or bad ways by friends?

That's why the Bible warns us to be careful of the friends we choose. Their influence tends to wear off on us—even if we don't think that's possible.

Do not be misled: "Bad company corrupts good character." (1 Cor. 15:33)

Solomon, the wisest man who ever lived, fell into this trap. He was told not to marry anyone who wasn't a dedicated follower of God because of the likelihood that she would cause him to compromise and become less dedicated to God than he was. But apparently, Solomon felt he was too strong and too smart to be in danger of being changed. So he married women who were not believers in God anyway. Some worshiped idols . . . and these women changed him.

King Solomon, however, loved many foreign women besides Pharaoh's daughter—Moabites, Ammonites, Edomites, Sidonians and Hittites. They were from nations about which the Lord had told the Israelites, "You must not intermarry with them, because they will surely turn your hearts after their gods." Nevertheless, Solomon held fast to them in love. He had seven hundred wives of royal birth and three hundred concubines, and his wives led him astray. As Solomon grew old, his wives turned his heart after other gods, and his heart was not fully devoted to the Lord his God, as the heart of David his father had been. He followed Ashtoreth the goddess of the Sidonians, and Molek the detestable god of the Ammonites. So Solomon did evil in the eyes of the LORD; he did not follow the LORD completely, as David his father had done. (1 Kings 11:1–6)

There are some people we follow online. Maybe they're celebrities, or athletes, or experts in some area. Maybe we respect them in some way, or admire their abilities. Do you think that even the people we hang around or follow in a virtual sense can possibly influence us—even those who don't know us?

Summing It Up

The iron was only in the solution for thirty minutes before change was obvious. Chances are, we're spending a lot more time with friends—or following online personalities—than that. Sometimes we think we're as strong as iron. Or we think the people we hang around with, even virtually, won't change us. But the truth is, they often do.

That's why we must be so careful about the friends we choose. Friends *will* influence us, for good or for bad. So let's seek friends—even those we follow virtually—who will help make us sharper and stronger followers of God. Does that make sense?

> As iron sharpens iron,
>   so one person sharpens another. (Prov. 27:17)

The company we keep matters. Sometimes the values of our friends or others we're around a lot rub off on us whether we want them to or not. And they stick—just like the copper did to the iron. Choose wisely.

Blowing Your Top

THEME: Giving unguarded vent to anger is bad, but so is stuffing it inside and not dealing with it. Pressure will build . . . and we're in for an explosion.

THINGS YOU'LL NEED

- ☐ *1-gallon sealable freezer bag*
- ☐ *2 cups vinegar*
- ☐ *1 cup warm water*
- ☐ *6 tablespoons baking soda*
- ☐ *Paper towels*
- ☐ *Safety glasses for everyone*
- ☐ *Permanent marker*

Advance Prep

This is designed to be done with the family outdoors, for obvious reasons. You'll definitely want to test this before doing it with the family. Make sure the gallon-size bags are freezer quality. They'll be a bit heavier duty—and the seams may hold better, which will tend to give a better *boom*.

1. Tear off a square of paper towel and pile the baking soda in the center. Now fold that paper towel loosely around the baking soda so you make a little pocket or envelope. Keep that to the side for the moment.

2. Draw a face—eyes, nose, mouth—on both sides of the plastic bag using the permanent marker. Use the whole bag . . . you want a big face.

3. Next, pour the warm water and vinegar into the empty bag.

4. Now, do the rest of this outside—if you're not there already.

5. Put on safety glasses.

6. Open the plastic bag and drop the pocket of baking soda into the water and vinegar solution. Combining these ingredients will create carbon dioxide gas, and we don't want to waste any of it. That is the purpose of folding it into the paper towel, which will give you a brief head start in sealing the bag before the baking soda itself hits the vinegar.

7. Seal the bag *quickly* and give it a fast shake to be sure the powder is mixing with the vinegar/water solution. The bag will start filling with gas immediately.

8. Quickly set the bag on the ground and back away, putting a little distance between you and the bag—unless you don't mind getting splattered a bit.

9. Once the bag fills and tightens, it will look like a giant head. When the pressure builds enough, the thing will burst open, blowing its top with a little *boom*.

Congratulations, you did it! Now clean up your mess, and you'll be ready to do this with the kids.

Running the Activity

Have each of the kids wear a pair of safety glasses. Whenever we're making something explode, safety glasses make a lot of sense. And even though this devotional isn't really all that dangerous, it will *feel* a bit more exciting if everyone is wearing the safety glasses.

Be sure to have the kids back a safe distance from the bag before you add the baking soda and seal it up. After the bag has exploded, you're ready to move on with the life lesson.

Teaching the Lesson

You've probably heard Mom or Dad come down on you a bit when you react in anger, right? What are some examples of ways we might sin when we're mad?

- Anger might cause us to say something rude, unkind, or harsh.
- We might even do something destructive or something that could hurt someone.

Self-control is a good thing, and we need it. But simply bottling up our anger isn't the answer either. We're not to hold on to it or stuff it down deep inside us. Why is that?

If the anger is still inside us, we can be like that plastic bag. Instead of filling with carbon dioxide, we're filling with resentment.

Bitterness. Unforgiveness. Impatience. If we don't deal with our anger in a healthy way, we'll blow our tops. Likely our anger is going to burst out suddenly . . . and make a real mess.

> "In your anger do not sin": Do not let the sun go down while you are still angry, and do not give the devil a foothold. (Eph. 4:26–27)

Lashing out in anger is bad, but so is holding on to the anger. We're not to bottle it up or just stuff it down deep and pretend it isn't there. Even though we may not say something nasty or do something hurtful in our anger, we don't want to hold on to it. According to the verse we just read, how fast do we need to deal with our anger?

What would be some appropriate ways to deal with our anger?

- Talk to Mom or Dad.
- Talk to the person we're angry with.
- Remind ourselves of some of the ways God has forgiven us when we didn't deserve it—and remember we're to forgive others the same way.
- Confess our anger to God and ask the Holy Spirit to change our hearts.
- All of the above.

Ephesians 4:26–27 warns us about a danger that comes when we don't deal with the anger quickly. What is it?

It is giving the devil a foothold. Just the word *giving* suggests we're handing him a huge advantage . . . and access into our lives. Making it easy for him. *Foothold*. Think of a climber. The purpose of a foothold is not to help a climber stay in that spot. A foothold is something a climber uses to move higher.

Think of a foothold in a military sense too. If an enemy gained a foothold in your territory, that would mean they've gained some control. The objective is always to use that foothold to advance farther and gain more ground . . . more control.

How might the devil get a foothold in our lives if we don't forgive or get over our anger quickly?

How might he advance from there to take more control of our lives?

How scary is that whole idea of the enemy controlling us at *any* level?

Summing It Up

Do you see why the Bible warns us to take care of anger quickly? If we don't, the enemy gets a foothold in our lives, and he'll advance from there. Likely the angry pressure will build and build until we say something we shouldn't or do something that is wrong and that we'll regret. We'll blow up somehow . . . and make a mess!

Is there any anger you're holding on to right now, something you need to deal with before the "sun goes down"?

Porn: Toxic. Twisting. Trap.

THEME: Pornography is wrong biblically and something to avoid. It is toxic, it twists those who embrace it, and it is a trap.

A Special Word for Parents

This lesson is the longest one in the entire book. Not the activity but just the things for you to read and consider. Read it. Pray about it. The lesson is longer because this is such a big danger for all our kids, and I don't want to just hit this at a surface level. I'm packing in a bit more information, perspective, and helps for parents so they can effectively talk to their kids about this issue.

 ⚠ **THINGS YOU'LL NEED**

- ☐ *Safety glasses* for all
- ☐ *Chemical-resistant gloves* for all

- ☐ *Sulfuric acid*, which is easily available in the plumbing aisle at the hardware store. I've used Rooto brand professional drain opener—which is basically concentrated sulfuric acid. I've also used Zep brand sulfuric acid drain opener, urgent, professional strength. You won't need much, so the quart bottle is more than enough.
- ☐ *2 clear drinking glasses*; a 16-ounce size is perfect. Pick them up at the dollar store or thrift store, because after you're done here, you won't want to drink anything out of them ever again.
- ☐ *Stir stick*, such as a short dowel rod or an unsharpened pencil
- ☐ *White sugar*, about a cup for each time you do the experiment

Advance Prep

First, let me remind you that use of porn is epidemic—and kids are getting exposed at younger and younger ages. Before you say, "Maybe I'll do this one when the kids are older," consider a few facts below.

- **Porn is addictive.** If your kids are exposed young, it is even more addictive.
- **Porn is damaging.** It will twist your kids' ideas of sex, the opposite sex, and tastes in both.
- **Kids are being exposed to porn at really young ages.** Do you have kids who are eight, nine, or ten years old? Likely they are much more aware of porn than you think they are. And at these ages they are very vulnerable to someone else who may expose them to porn. Protect them by going over this with them.

You're a good parent. Likely you have one of these concerns below. Let's talk about them quickly.

Won't I build their curiosity about porn? Not if you show them that it is a trap to avoid. You'd surely warn your kids at a very young age not to play with handguns. Think of porn as being just as deadly . . . and protect your kids.

What if some of my kids are old enough to address this topic but some are not? Don't miss talking to your older kids because of the younger ones. You can separate them and do this just for the older kids. Or leave the younger ones in the devotion, and just address the older ones in the teaching time. If they are truly too young for it, they won't follow what you're saying. No worries. If they do understand even part of what you say, then maybe they aren't too young after all.

What if I don't feel qualified to teach on the topic because I've struggled with porn myself? Then you know some of the dangers firsthand, and your job is to protect your kids. Don't let the enemy make you think you're "disqualified" somehow. He wants your kids unprotected and vulnerable.

Okay. Hopefully you're ready to proceed, and this is definitely one you'll want to practice before doing it with the kids.

1. Choose a place outdoors to practice. The solution will get hot, so keep that in mind. And the steam rising off the solution will smell horrible. Be careful you are not in the path of those vapors, and you don't want to be so close to the house that the fumes can drift inside. They smell nasty, and a whiff at close range can make you gag.
2. Fill one clear glass about halfway with sugar (about 1 cup).
3. Put on your safety glasses and gloves. And if you wear prescription glasses and don't think you need safety glasses . . . put them on anyway.

4. Add some sulfuric acid to the glass of sugar. You won't need much. Start with about half an inch.

5. With the glass solidly on the ground, hold the glass firmly in place with one gloved hand and stir the sugar/sulfuric acid solution using the stir stick in the other. You want to create a thick, slushy consistency. If you have pockets of dry sugar, add a bit more sulfuric acid.

6. The solution should get hot and begin changing color. First it will be an amber color. Then the color of iced tea. Finally, it will get black and tar-like. At this point stop stirring and remove the stir stick. Remember, by the time this turns black, it will be hot. You may even see bubbles popping at the surface.

7. Step away from the glass. Steamy vapors will rise that are absolutely pungent. This stuff is nasty smelling enough to make you gag or make your eyes water.

8. The tar-like solution will expand and rise out of the glass like a giant black snake.

9. When it stops, remember it is still hot.

10. Give it plenty of time to cool, then inspect it. The solution has turned into a dark column almost like Styrofoam.

You're ready to do this with the kids!

Running the Activity

Be sure all of the kids are wearing safety glasses and that you are doing this outdoors. You, along with anyone helping you, should be wearing chemical-resistant gloves.

Now do the experiment with the sugar and sulfuric acid just as you practiced. If one of the kids is old enough to stir the solution responsibly, that would be great. Just watch closely so you know when to tell them to stop and back away. They do not want to inhale the steam that will rise from the solution.

Once the black column has risen, let the glass cool as you teach the lesson.

> I'm going into the type of detail I'd use for teenagers here. You can scale it back to an age appropriate level for your kids. Remember, they are probably more ready for this than you might think. And the risk of too much information now is often better than not giving them adequate information so they can make wise choices.

Teaching the Lesson

We started out with pure sugar. Brainstorm with me for a moment. What are some things that we make taste better—and are so much more enjoyable—by adding sugar?

It isn't only cake and cookies and other treats that taste better with sugar. Even ketchup contains sugar, and without it you may not want it on your fries like you do now.

God designed sex in marriage to be kind of like that pure, clean sugar. Something that sweetens life. Sometimes people make sex seem like it is a dirty thing, but God created it to be good—when it is limited to marriage.

What do you think are the two main reasons God created sex?

- To populate the earth.
- To draw a married couple close together in love.

What might be some ways sex sweetens marriage?

- It strengthens the couple in emotional and physical ways.
- It promotes trust between the couple.
- It rekindles passionate love.
- It reminds the couple how much they need each other.
- It tends to make worries, problems, and the stress of the day melt away.

That's how God designed sex in marriage—with lots of benefits.

If ranking the importance of sex in marriage from 1 to 10, many married couples would rank sex right up there as a 9 or 10. If it is that important, is it any wonder that our enemy would try to mess up God's plan for sex in marriage? And one big way he does this is to expose kids to porn.

The sulfuric acid represents what porn will do to the pureness of sex the way God designed it to be.

How might viewing porn mess up your chances of having good sex later, after you're married?

- **Pornography is a trap because it is highly addictive.** Viewing porn releases chemicals in the brain—and the body craves it more and more often. Addiction happens long before most people realize. Addictions to porn are as hard to break as drug addictions. Those who get into porn go into marriage with that addiction. When their spouse finds out, huge problems of trust, shame, and so much more threaten the health of their marriage.
- **Pornography twists the viewer's tastes.** Sex between a husband and wife is about expressing pure love. Porn is about expressing pure lust. Often the porn viewer will get appetites for things they would have never imagined otherwise.

- **Pornography gives false expectations.** Porn promotes selfish sex and gives a false expectation about what sex will be like when you're married. This can lead to huge problems in marriage.
- **Pornography separates you from the real world.** Porn will often cause people to prefer the imaginary world of pornography over having sex with their spouse. That is twisted.
- **Pornography will push you to live out twisted fantasies.** That chemical high from watching porn will require more and more to get the same high.

Summing It Up

Pornography, like that sulfuric acid, will take the beauty of good, pure sex in marriage and make it into something dark and twisted.

I'm pleading with you to avoid pornography in all its forms. Pictures. Movies. Online. In print.

Listen to what the Bible says about avoiding this type of thing—about staying away from the types of people who make and participate in pornography.

> Now then, my sons, listen to me;
>   pay attention to what I say.
> Do not let your heart turn to her ways
>   or stray into her paths.
> Many are the victims she has brought down;
>   her slain are a mighty throng.
> Her house is a highway to the grave,
>   leading down to the chambers of death. (Prov. 7:24–27)

Are you catching that? This talks about "her house is a highway to the grave, leading down to the chambers of death." And when you view pornography, you are going to her house.

Sulfuric acid is toxic. Poison. You saw what it did to the sugar. You would never drink sulfuric acid. You'd never let it inside your body, would you? Porn is just as toxic. Just as poisonous. Avoid it at all costs. It will hurt you now and rob you of so much of God's good plan for sex after you get married.

A Special Word for Parents

This was a heavy topic but so essential for you to talk to the kids about . . . for their protection. Now, you may want to follow this up with one-on-one talks with each of your kids. If they are older, there is a good chance they've been exposed to porn—and may still be involved with it.

Current or Past Porn Exposure

- Ask them about that. Remember, they may be carrying some guilt and shame. And if they are currently into porn, they may not be honest with you, just like a drug addict would attempt to deceive.
- Ask if it is something they still get involved in from time to time, or ask when the last time they saw porn was.
- If they admit to being involved in porn in any way, ask them if they want to be free of it. Then lead them in how to do that. The testimony we hear from most who are into porn is that the battle is hard and takes a long time.

How to Break Free from Pornography

- Realize how are they accessing porn. What can you do to eliminate that access? Can you get them a different phone without full internet capabilities, or eliminate the phone? Can you keep phones and other devices out of their bedroom—especially at night?
- They need to want to be free. It has to be their heart's desire. If it is only your desire to see them free, you'll be a cop—and they'll keep looking for ways to outmaneuver you.

- They need to ask the Holy Spirit to help them—to change their heart. To give them new desires. Praying for God's help this way is an extremely effective tool in our Christian tool belt.
- They need to be in the Word. Especially passages that remind them of how wrong porn use is. Here are a few starting points: Proverbs 4:14–15; 5:3–13; 5:20–23; 6:25–26; Galatians 5:16–17.
- They need to make changes. Maybe their friends are encouraging this. Find out. And together with your kids, map out changes that can help distance them from temptations.
- Accountability and filters are okay, but they are the weaker tools on the tool belt. If their heart isn't dedicated to breaking free, they will always find a way to be deceptive on this. But still, filters are a good idea. Covenant Eyes is one I've heard that many use.
- Pray for your kids. And keep your eyes on this situation. Can we turn that black column of sulfuric acid and sugar back to pure sugar again? No. Only God can do that. And in the same way, we can't undo the damage porn has already done in our kids. Only God can do that—but as we rely on him, remember, he *can* do that.

Vacuum-Packed

THEME: Fear can paralyze us, but God can help us conquer fear!

 ## THINGS YOU'LL NEED

- ☐ *Small vacuum* with flexible hose attachment. A wet/dry or shop vac works just fine.
- ☐ *Extra large, clear plastic trash bag* at least 1 mil. thick. The type used to bag up leaves and yard waste. A 50-gallon bag is ideal and should be available at your hardware store. A clear bag is great, but a black bag will do as well.

Advance Prep

If you don't have a vacuum with a flexible hose, be sure to allow enough time to do some calling around to borrow or buy one.

Now, you'll want to test this before trying it with the kids. Get another couple of parents together and run through this. Ideally, you'll need three people to pull off a good test run on this. Open the plastic bag and set it on the floor, seam to the ground. Push the sides down and bunch them so you make a large oval out of the open bag on the floor.

Person 1

1. This person takes off their shoes and kneels down in the bag. Have them kneel low, so they are sitting back on their heels. This should *not* be a person who is at all claustrophobic.
2. Raise the bag around them, stopping at their shoulders or just *below* their neck. Remember, don't raise the bag over anybody's head—not ever—not even as a joke. And you should not even have to raise the bag to their neck.
3. Their hands and arms should be inside the bag.

Person 2

1. This person will handle the vacuum, turning it off and on and feeding the flexible hose to Person 1. The best position is directly behind the person in the bag.
2. They'll want to feed the hose over the shoulder of the person in the bag so that the end is somewhere around chest or stomach level for Person 1.

Person 3

1. This is the person who is watching everything . . . the person in control. This is the position I always take, and I would suggest you take this spot too. Person 3 instructs Person 1 to use their hand as a type of extended screen over the open end of the

vacuum hose. Person 1 must keep the plastic bag from getting sucked up in the hose, which would block this little experiment from working.

2. Person 3 gathers up the slack at the bag opening so that the bag is snug around the shoulders and collar bone of the person kneeling in the bag.

3. This person instructs the person controlling the vacuum on when to flip the switch—and when to turn it off.

4. Once the vacuum is on, it will quickly suck the air out of the bag so that the bag clings tightly to the body of Person 1. If this doesn't happen, make sure the mouth of the bag is sealed well against their body and that the bag isn't clogging the vacuum hose.

5. You'll know if you're doing this right if the bag clings tight to the volunteer, appearing to "vacuum-pack" them. They should not be able to stand or even raise their hands. Terrific!

6. Instruct Person 2 to turn the vacuum off as soon as the bag appears to vacuum-pack your volunteer—or sooner if Person 1 looks fearful or wants to stop.

Running the Activity

Run through the activity just as you practiced. You'll know when the vacuum gets the air out of the bag by the way it clings to Person 1. At this point, you may want to test how well the bag is holding them in place by asking a question or two.

Can you stand up?

Can you raise your arms—for twenty dollars?

If you've done it right, you won't be losing any money on this one. Now turn off the vacuum and let your volunteer out of the bag. You're ready to teach the lesson.

Teaching the Lesson

Our volunteer could not raise their arms or stand. Was it the vacuum holding them in place or the plastic bag?

Actually, neither. The bag is not all that thick. You could poke a hole in it with your finger. And if you put the palm of your hand on the end of the vacuum nozzle right now and we turned it on, you could pull away easily.

Atmospheric pressure is the thing that kept our volunteer from breaking free. The vacuum only sucked the air out of the bag. Once it did, this allowed atmospheric pressure to press down on that bag covering their body—at 14.7 pounds per square inch. No wonder they couldn't stand!

This is a picture of the way fear can impact us in life. Sometimes fear can keep us from moving forward. Fear is powerful and can't be seen—just like atmospheric pressure. Fear can paralyze us and hold us in place.

Sometimes fear is good. It keeps us from doing something foolish . . . something that will get us hurt.

Can you give an example of when good fear might keep us safe?

Other times fear is bad, keeping us from doing the things God would want us to do.

Can you give examples of how fear can hold us back from doing good things?

How can we get over that bad fear—the fear that keeps us para-lyzed and unable to do the things we know we should do?

Ultimately, God can help us to function even when we are afraid. Here are some things that may help. Remember:

- **If you are a follower of Christ, God will never leave you.** That means you aren't doing this alone.

> "Never will I leave you;
>   never will I forsake you."

So we say with confidence,

> "The Lord is my helper; I will not be afraid.
> What can mere mortals do to me?" (Heb. 13:5–6)

- **God really cares about you, and he wants you to trust him with your fears.**

Cast all your anxiety on him because he cares for you. (1 Pet. 5:7)

- **Even the bravest of people face fear.** We can learn from them how to handle fear. Listen to what King David wrote—a mighty warrior who faced fear many times.

> When I am afraid, I put my trust in you.
>   In God, whose word I praise—
> in God I trust and am not afraid.
>   What can mere mortals do to me? (Ps. 56:3–4)

Summing It Up

Sometimes fear is good. It keeps us from things that can hurt us. It keeps us from taking unnecessary and dangerous risks.

Other times fear is bad. It paralyzes us and keeps us from doing what we should. It's at those times we want to put our faith in God in a fresh way and press ahead. If we do, then I think that even bad fear can be turned into something good—because it drives us closer to Jesus!

Reaching Friends in Darkness

THEME: We must be a light—a good example of what a Christian is—if we want to reach our friends in darkness.

 THINGS YOU'LL NEED

- ☐ *Povidone iodine.* An 8-ounce bottle works great and is available over the counter at any pharmacy. Ideally, pick up two bottles so you can use one for practice.
- ☐ *Chlorine neutralizer* (sodium sulfite), available at any pool supply store. Often it comes in a 3-pound container, but you won't need much, so buy a smaller quantity if they stock it. The brand I used is Leslie's Swimming Pool Supplies.
- ☐ *Small (penlight) flashlight*
- ☐ *Turkey baster,* one with a clear plastic applicator portion. You'll want to slide the rubber squeeze ball off the end and insert the flashlight instead so the plastic applicator works sort of like a light saber.

- [ ] *Bucket of water, no more than 3 gallons.* A large, clear glass bowl works even better—or if you had access to a small fish aquarium, that would be even more impressive.
- [ ] *Stir stick.* A wooden spoon or paint stir stick works fine.
- [ ] *Duct tape*
- [ ] *Safety glasses* for everyone
- [ ] *Chemical-resistant gloves* for you or anyone handling the chemical end of things. The sodium sulfite crystals are an irritant.
- [ ] *Silicone* to seal the narrow end of the baster
- [ ] *Glass of water*

Note: You're going to use this same object lesson here as in Activity 38, Christmas: We Don't Have to Be Scared of the Dark Anymore, but each will have an entirely different application. So as you're collecting supplies, realize you'll need all these same things again.

Advance Prep

Yes, there are a few things you'll need to pick up in advance to do this devotional. But don't let that stop you. The family will *love* this activity, which means you'll be giving them biblical truth in a powerful way. Don't skip this one!

Before you do this, take a blob of silicone and seal the narrow end of the baster. You'll need to give this time to dry, preferably overnight.

Now, practice this little chemical reaction in advance—if for no other reason than you'll be a bit smoother when you do it with the family. And, hey, this is so fun you'll want to do it more than once anyway.

1. Slip on a pair of safety glasses, then add the iodine to the water in the bucket/bowl/aquarium. Use the stir stick to mix the iodine in evenly. The water will turn very dark.
2. Slip the rubber squeeze bulb off the baster, and duct-tape the flashlight in its place so the light will shine through the clear plastic applicator.
3. Start to stir the water with the clear plastic applicator.
4. Add about 1 tablespoon of the chlorine neutralizer crystals to the water while stirring. Ideally, you'll want to make this a subtle move on your part. Your objective is to add the powder in such a way the kids don't notice.
5. The water will grow lighter. Continue stirring until the water is clear.

I'll bet you'll be smiling when the dark water turns beautifully clear again. Amazing, right? That's exactly what your family will think too! But this was your practice run . . . and we'll do it a little differently with the family. We won't add the neutralizer until after we've started teaching the lesson.

Running the Activity

Have the water ready with the iodine already mixed in the bucket/bowl/aquarium before you bring in the kids. Have a glass of water to the side filled with the same dark iodine water.

Ask your kids if they can make the water clear again. Likely they'll admit they can't. Next, ask one of them to pour in the iodine liquid from the extra glass. Did that help do anything to lighten the dark water in the bucket?

Teaching the Lesson

The water in the large bucket represents friends of ours who aren't saved. Their hearts are still darkened by sin. Can we change their hearts . . . clean them up? No. That's a job only God can do. But we can help—or hurt—the process.

When we added the dark water, that certainly didn't help clear up the water. How might we actually contribute to the sin and darkness already in the heart of a friend? If we are not living out our lives as a Christian should—if we are a bad example of what a Christian should be like—can you see how that might be adding darkness to our friend's life?

Now turn on the flashlight and stir the water—while casually adding the neutralizer (without them noticing, if possible). You may ask one of the kids to take the light and do the stirring.

As soon as the water turns clear, you're ready to move on.

When we added the light to the water, then the water cleared up.

The Bible reminds us to live in such a way that we're an example to others of how a follower of Jesus should live. First Timothy 4:12 tells of five broad areas in which we need to be an example to others: in speech (how we talk), in conduct (how we behave), in love, in faith, and in purity. How can we be a light that shows our friends the love of Christ in some of these areas?

- **Talk nicely** to parents, brothers and sisters, and others.
- **Treat others nicely**—the way we'd like to be treated.
- **Tell the truth**, even if it means we'll get in big trouble.
- **Do the right thing** even when nobody else does . . . or nobody else is looking.
- **Encourage others or notice others.** Sometimes just smiling and saying hi is all it takes.

- **Learn to pray and read your Bible** to become more like Jesus.
- **Trust God enough to live the way he tells us to live in the Bible;** in other words, do what the Bible says.

These are just some ways we can be a light in a dark world. What are some other ways?

If we lived this way more consistently, might some of our friends be attracted to the light of our life?

Summing It Up

Jesus is the Light of the World. He is the one who can forgive sins and change hearts. He is the one who leads us out of darkness and into the light. Jesus put it this way:

I am the light of the world. Whoever follows me will never walk in darkness, but will have the light of life. (John 8:12)

The apostle Paul put it like this:

He has rescued us from the dominion of darkness and brought us into the kingdom of the Son he loves. (Col. 1:13)

The way we live can either hurt what Jesus would like to do in the hearts of our friends—or help.

Let's help bring the light of Jesus to our friends at church, school, the neighborhood, or wherever else we are.

For you were once darkness, but now you are light in the Lord. Live as children of light. (Eph. 5:8)

Christmas: We Don't Have to Be Scared of the Dark Anymore

THEME: We don't have to be afraid of the dark, because the Light of the World has come.

 ⚠️ **THINGS YOU'LL NEED**

You're going to use this same object lesson here as in Activity 37, Reaching Friends in Darkness, but each will have an entirely different application. See the previous devotional for the list of Things You'll Need, as well as for the Advance Prep and the Running the Activity sections of that lesson.

Advance Prep

See note above.

Running the Activity

See note above.

Teaching the Lesson

Now light a candle and turn off the lights for a bit. This is just about helping create a mood—and it will also help hide what you're doing when you add the chlorine neutralizer to the water.

What is it about the dark that scares people so much?

Why is it that a place we enjoy or love in the daylight can become creepy and scary in the dark? Can you think of any examples?

Basements are often fun with all the lights on . . . but in the dark? No thanks.

The woods or a forest preserve makes a nice picnic spot in the daytime, but at night—with maybe a coyote howling in the distance?

Our own home is a place where we feel safe and secure. But when all the lights are off, does that feeling change a bit?

Imagine a county fair or carnival. Lots of fun, right? But what if you cut all the lights—and had to walk through the place alone at night? It's probably not going to be as much fun.

I think the dark, or darkness, is closely related to evil and sin in our minds. Darkness is often equated with all things bad. If a story starts with the words, "It was a dark and stormy night," we're already figuring something bad is going to happen.

Darkness is just plain scary. The fact that we can't see where we're going—or who or what might be there in the dark to jump out at us—can make us really afraid.

Hell has been described as a place of darkness, so it's no wonder that deep inside each of us is a natural fear of the dark.

Who is the one person or being that is the darkest, scariest of all? The devil has been described as the prince of darkness. Yes, something deep inside us knows that darkness is not where we want to be.

But that is part of the wonder and joy of Christmas—it means we don't have to live in darkness anymore. Listen to how some of these verses describe Jesus and what it meant when he came into this world.

> When Jesus spoke again to the people, he said, "I am the light of the world. Whoever follows me will never walk in darkness, but will have the light of life. (John 8:12)

> I have come into the world as a light, so that no one who believes in me should stay in darkness. (12:46)

Jesus is light, and he came to rescue us from darkness. No wonder we love putting Christmas lights everywhere . . . as a reminder of the light of the world who came to save us.

Finish the iodine water demonstration. Slip the flashlight you've attached in the baster into the water—along with the neutralizer crystals or powder. Remember, this is when you want to really be subtle with how you get the neutralizer into the bucket/bowl/aquarium. Ideally, they'll never even notice you adding it.

Stir the neutralizer crystals into the water with the baster/flashlight contraption until all evidence of the iodine is gone. You may

want to blow out the candle and turn on the lights so everyone can
see how clear the water really is.

Summing It Up

If we are followers of Jesus, we have been rescued from an eternity of darkness and from the darkness of this world. That is the message of Christmas.

> The people walking in darkness
>   have seen a great light;
> on those living in the land of deep darkness
>   a light has dawned. (Isa. 9:2)

And if we have been rescued from darkness, we need to live in gratitude to our Jesus and in obedience to him.

> For you were once darkness, but now you are light in the Lord. Live as children of light. (Eph. 5:8)

We don't have to be scared of the dark anymore—or the prince of darkness. The message of Christmas is that Jesus has saved us from darkness, and that is something we can celebrate all year long!

Christmas: So Close, but Yet So Far

Making the effort to seek out Jesus personally.

THINGS YOU'LL NEED

No real supplies needed, except for a little cash for a snack.

Advance Prep

You'll need to find a destination about six miles from your house. That distance is important. And be sure it's someplace the kids would really like to go. A fast-food place generally works great. You may also go to a park or museum or some other place you can do an activity with the kids, if you'd rather.

Running the Activity

I'm going to talk you through this as if you were going to a fast-food place. Think Chick-fil-A or Wendy's. Somewhere you can get a little something for dessert for each of the kids.

You'll want them to feel the reward was well worth the drive, so keep that in mind when you're picking a destination. And remember that goal when you tell them what they can order on the menu. Maybe, instead of a snack, consider letting them order a meal. Or adding a shake to their order. That would work really well.

After the kids are sitting at the table with their snack or food, you're ready to start the teaching time.

Teaching the Lesson

We drove six miles to get here. What do you think; was it worth the drive?

Actually, we could have walked this distance in a couple of hours at an easy pace. We probably would have been hungrier—and I'd have bought more food if we did. But what do you think? Could you have done that?

I'm pretty sure we could've all made the walk if the destination on the other end was important enough to us. And this has some similarities to the story of Jesus's birth in the Bible, especially the part about the Magi (wise men) who came to worship Jesus.

> After Jesus was born in Bethlehem in Judea, during the time of King Herod, Magi from the east came to Jerusalem and asked, "Where is the one who has been born king of the Jews? We saw his star when it rose and have come to worship him."
>
> When King Herod heard this he was disturbed, and all Jerusalem with him. When he had called together all the people's chief priests

and teachers of the law, he asked them where the Messiah was to be born. "In Bethlehem in Judea," they replied. (Matt. 2:1–5)

The Magi explained that they'd seen a star that showed the Messiah had been born. And the religious leaders answered the big question of where this was supposed to happen: in Bethlehem, which was only about six miles away.

> Besides clueing in the Magi as to what town the Messiah was to be born in, what else did the religious leaders do?
> Did they actually do anything or make any effort to meet Jesus personally?

The priests and teachers had been hoping for the Messiah to come, but now that they heard he had arrived, they made zero effort to go meet him for themselves. They could have walked the distance in a couple hours, and if they'd hopped on a donkey or camel, they could have gotten to Bethlehem even more quickly.

> Their lack of effort to meet Jesus . . . what does that say about how eager they really were for the Messiah?

Maybe they thought, *Well, Bethlehem is so close. I can go there anytime.* Or maybe they were too busy with friends at the moment. But the point is, they didn't go. Not one of them.

> What price did they pay by not personally going to meet Jesus?

Ultimately, they missed out and made mistakes that cost them something huge in their lifetime—and most of them missed heaven for all eternity too. And all because they didn't make the effort to seek Jesus when they had the chance.

- **Jesus wasn't in Bethlehem long after that.** Soon after the Magi visited Bethlehem, King Herod plotted to kill Jesus. An angel warned Joseph to take Mary and Jesus away from Bethlehem and escape to Egypt. So even if the religious leaders had decided to check out Bethlehem a week after the Magi visited, they wouldn't have found Jesus. They missed their opportunity. It wasn't until after King Herod died that Joseph moved his family back—but they settled in Nazareth of Galilee, not Bethlehem.

- **Because they didn't seek Jesus in Bethlehem, they missed the fact that his birth fulfilled the prophecies about the Messiah.** Years later, when adult Jesus was preaching and teaching, the religious leaders just couldn't or wouldn't accept the fact that he was the Messiah. One of their hang-ups? They'd heard Jesus was from Nazareth and had grown up there. They assumed he'd been born there too—which was a huge mistake. The leaders knew the Scriptures taught that the true Messiah would be born in Bethlehem. If the leaders had made that short little trip to Bethlehem when Jesus was born, they would have seen the whole picture. They would have realized he was the Messiah—and it would have changed their lives both on earth and for all eternity.

They were so close . . . only six miles away. But they were so far too. They missed Jesus for all time.

Summing It Up

The leaders didn't make an effort to meet with Jesus themselves to see if he really was the Messiah. How can that happen to us?

- Sometimes we don't make the effort to meet with Jesus personally.

- We don't put any effort into spending time with him.
- We are content with letting somebody else meet with Jesus (like a pastor), expecting they'll tell us about what they learned. That is just like King Herod. He sent the Magi to meet Jesus—but told them to come back and fill him in.

How many of you enjoyed our little snack just now?

How would you have liked it if I came here and snacked without you and just told you about how good it was? That wouldn't help you one bit, would it?

Our little six-mile trip today was all about helping you remember to put the effort into meeting with Jesus.

- Don't rely solely on pastors telling you what they've learned about Jesus.
- Don't be content to settle for just what Mom or Dad tells you about Jesus.

Each of us must meet with Jesus individually. Each of us has to put in the effort to have a relationship with him. Sometimes that means we have to put down our screens, or whatever we are busy with, to do the work of getting to know Jesus for ourselves. Doing so will benefit you now—and I guarantee it will benefit you even more later.

Easter: The Cross Most Never See

THEME: The cross was much more than a cruel way to kill Jesus. It was a weapon that Jesus used to defeat sin and death.

THINGS YOU'LL NEED

- ☐ *5-gallon bucket filled with sand*, or even better, access to a sandbox or beach
- ☐ *Two wood crosses* representing the crosses on either side of Jesus
- ☐ *One more wood cross with a longer upright section that resembles a sword.* Or, as an easy option, pick up a toy sword, but you'll have to wrap it with aluminum foil so it isn't obvious that it is a sword when the kids first see it.

Advance Prep

You can get help on this. Don't let the idea of making crosses or a sword keep you from doing this devotional. Ask around at church. You'll likely have no trouble finding someone who would love to help.

1. *Make the two crosses.* Don't make this hard. All you're doing is nailing, screwing, or gluing some 1 × 2 inch strips of wood together.
2. *Make the sword.* Use the same 1 × 2 strips as the other crosses, but use a longer piece for the upright section. Cut the long end so it forms a point like a sword. If you buy a toy sword instead of making one from wood, wrap aluminum foil around the sword hilt and guard, and the part of the blade that will not be buried in the sand.

Determine where you'll do this devotional. If it is in a bucket with sand, practice sinking the three crosses in the bucket in such a way that the kids will never guess one is a sword. You'll be driving the sword cross deeper into the sand than you do the others so they all appear to be the same height.

Running the Activity

Have the crosses in the sand *before* the kids come into the room or join you at the sandbox or beach. We don't want them to have any clue that one of the crosses is really a sword. The sword should be positioned between the other two crosses.

You'll move right into teaching the lesson at this point. The activity of "revealing" the sword comes later.

Teaching the Lesson

When he had received the drink, Jesus said, "It is finished." With that, he bowed his head and gave up his spirit. (John 19:30)

On the cross, Jesus said, "It is finished." People thought it was the end of Jesus. That he was beaten. But what was Jesus talking about? What did he complete or finish by dying on the cross?

- **Doing God's will.** "For I have come down from heaven not to do my will but to do the will of him who sent me" (John 6:38).
- **Delivering God's message to the people.** "For I did not speak on my own, but the Father who sent me commanded me to say all that I have spoken" (12:49).
- **Telling people God's truth.** "In fact, the reason I was born and came into the world is to testify to the truth" (18:37).
- **Bringing a fuller life to people.** "The thief comes only to steal and kill and destroy; I have come that they may have life, and have it to the full" (10:10).
- **Providing a way to save the world.** "I did not come to judge the world, but to save the world" (12:47).
- **Calling sinners to repentance.** "I have not come to call the righteous, but sinners to repentance" (Luke 5:32).
- **Seeking and saving the lost.** "For the Son of Man came to seek and to save the lost" (19:10).
- **Proclaiming good news.** "The Spirit of the Lord is on me, because he has anointed me to proclaim good news to the poor. He has sent me to proclaim freedom for the prisoners and recovery of sight for the blind, to set the oppressed free, to proclaim the year of the Lord's favor" (4:18–19).
- **Glorifying God's name.** "Now my soul is troubled, and what shall I say? 'Father, save me from this hour'? No, it was for

this very reason I came to this hour. Father, glorify your name!" (John 12:27–28).

- **Making eternal life available to all.** "For God so loved the world that he gave his one and only Son, that whoever believes in him shall not perish but have eternal life" (3:16).

When Jesus said "It is finished," he was saying so much more than people realized at the time. Jesus *finished* all these things we just listed above—and more—with his death on the cross.

Jesus also *defeated* some things on the cross. He finished them off. Anybody know what he defeated? Death, the penalty of sin, and the devil.

He has saved us and called us to a holy life—not because of anything we have done but because of his own purpose and grace. This grace was given us in Christ Jesus before the beginning of time, but it has now been revealed through the appearing of our Savior, Christ Jesus, who has destroyed death and has brought life and immortality to light through the gospel. (2 Tim. 1:9–10)

When you were dead in your sins and in the uncircumcision of your flesh, God made you alive with Christ. He forgave us all our sins, having canceled the charge of our legal indebtedness, which stood against us and condemned us; he has taken it away, nailing it to the cross. And having disarmed the powers and authorities, he made a public spectacle of them, triumphing over them by the cross. (Col. 2:13–15)

The verses above talk about Jesus disarming the powers and authorities. This certainly includes removing the devil's weapons. The devil was defeated . . . disarmed of his weapons against us. He can no longer condemn those who put their faith in Jesus. The debt of our sin was paid on the cross.

So in reality, the cross wasn't just a cross. It was a weapon, like a giant sword.

Now is the time for you or one of the kids to pull out that middle cross (and take off the aluminum foil if you used it). You want the kids to see the sword now, for the first time.

Nobody knew fully what Jesus was really doing when he gave himself up as a sacrifice. Nobody actually realized what all he'd finished—or what he was finishing off.

- His disciples didn't know.
- His mom didn't know.
- The guards didn't know.
- The government officials didn't know.
- The religious leaders didn't know.

Jesus wasn't defeated on the cross. He was the one who did the defeating. By dying on the cross, Jesus completed the ultimate rescue mission to save us from death, sin, and the devil.

> For he has rescued us from the dominion of darkness and brought us into the kingdom of the Son he loves, in whom we have redemption, the forgiveness of sins. (Col. 1:13–14)

Summing It Up

When Jesus said "It is finished," he had done more for us than anybody realized.

Jesus *accomplished*. He finished all the Father sent him to do. And he finished off the things that we could never have beaten ourselves: sin, death, and the devil.

Now that we really see all that Jesus finished—and finished off for us—how grateful should we be, and how much more should that make us want to serve him with our whole heart?

Fourth of July: Freedom Worth Celebrating

THEME: The freedoms we enjoy in this nation are wonderful, yet the freedom Jesus earned for us is far greater . . . and something we should celebrate much more than we do.

 THINGS YOU'LL NEED

☐ *Fireworks.* Get the most interesting or spectacular ones you feel comfortable with. There's a great variety of things that blow up, light up, and bring excitement to any Fourth of July celebration. Some of the small tanks and spinning helicopters are pretty tame, but they're still fun too—and don't forget the sparklers! The key is to get some variety that all your kids will enjoy.

☐ *Lighter.* The long-snouted stick type is best for lighting those wicks.

☐ *Safety glasses* for all who will be present

☐ *Ear protection* (optional) is your call, but some of those bangs aren't so great on the ears. Foam earplugs from the pharmacy are cheap and may help prevent hearing problems down the line.

Advance Prep

Pick up the fireworks—and you'll want to do this well in advance to get a great selection. You can also ask around church, work, or the neighborhood to see if someone has a stash they are willing to share—or if they'll be driving through those states that have firework retail warehouses right along the main routes. You can give them some cash to pick some up for you while they travel.

Running the Activity

1. Go over the safety rules with the kids about staying a safe distance away, not rushing in to see why a wick on a firework went out, never relighting a short wick that went out before activating the fireworks, being really aware of what they're doing, keeping their safety glasses on, and so forth.
2. Also add ear protection, if you choose.
3. The person lighting the fireworks must pick a spot that is safely clear of any houses, parked cars, and especially people.
4. Now have fun blowing up the fireworks!

Teaching the Lesson

There are various dates that carry a special meaning to citizens of our country. Dates that many celebrate because they remind them of specific freedoms or of an independence associated with that date.

- January 1, 1863: "Emancipation Proclamation," celebrating President Lincoln's executive order declaring all slaves—even in the Confederate States—to be free.
- May 5, 1862: "Cinco de Mayo," originally marking Mexico's victory over France, has evolved into a day celebrating freedom, culture, and heritage in many areas of the States.
- May 30, 1955: "Memorial Day," a day designated by President Eisenhower to remember soldiers who gave their lives to help keep America free and safe from enemies.
- June 19, 1865: "Juneteenth," celebrating the order delivered by Union army general Gordon Granger that declared freedom for slaves in Texas.
- July 4, 1776: "Fourth of July," celebrating when the Declaration of Independence was approved by the Continental Congress.

For the purposes of the illustration, I'll use the example of July 4 to teach the lesson. If one of these other dates/celebrations would be more meaningful to you or your family, simply swap it out.

There may be no single date that resonates with every person in the country, but let's pick July 4 to illustrate today's truth, okay? People all over this country celebrate the day by shooting off fireworks—like we just did.

But let's take a step back. Exactly what are we celebrating on the Fourth of July?

What is now known as the United States of America used to be ruled by a king. And for many reasons, the people felt this king was a tyrant—doing things that were hard on the people living here. So the people back then revolted, and at the end of a very hard-fought

Revolutionary War, they gained independence. A freedom that we continue to enjoy in many ways.

What are some of the freedoms we have because this country's forebears fought for independence?

- **Freedom to worship** God or not as we choose.
- **Freedom to vote** on who will lead us rather than a royal family continuing to rule us for years and years and years.
- **Freedom to have a fair trial** if we're accused of a crime.
- **Freedom of speech** to express our opinions and beliefs and views.
- **Freedom to assemble** to gather together for whatever reason.
- **Freedom of the press** so newspapers and reporters can share facts and opinions about things—including negative views of our government and officials.

We could go on and on. We enjoy massive amounts of freedom in our country, and there are definitely many things we can celebrate and thank God for.

As Christians, there is another freedom that goes infinitely beyond any national holiday. It certainly completely eclipses anything our country won in the Revolutionary War. Anybody want to guess what that is all about?

All of humankind were slaves to sin . . . in a prison of sorts. And we were all subject to a ruler who was an absolute tyrant, the one the Bible refers to as "the king of terrors" in Job 18:14.

We were all doomed to perish and spend eternity in hell, with no way to escape. But God had a plan.

For God so loved the world that he gave his one and only Son, that whoever believes in him shall not perish but have eternal life. (John 3:16)

Through him everyone who believes is set free from every sin. (Acts 13:39)

Jesus paid the price for our sin and purchased our freedom. He made us truly free.

- We are freed from spending eternity in hell.
- We are freed from a life that is essentially enslavement to the king of terrors.

And he made us free to love and to serve him—and to do the things God put us on this earth to do.

For the Fourth of July, we celebrate a freedom that brings us benefits here in this life. People often celebrate with picnics, barbeques, parties, and fireworks. Many workers get a day off work, with pay. If we do all that to celebrate something that is temporary, how much more should we be celebrating the freedom Jesus gave us, which benefits us for all eternity?

Summing It Up

The Fourth of July is definitely something to celebrate. But let's not forget to celebrate all year round how Christ has saved us from the tyranny of sin and the king of terrors. He made his true followers free . . . not just for now but for all eternity.

How does that make you want to serve him better and live for him more?

What do you say we blow off some more fireworks—and give thanks to God for his great plan and for Jesus's great sacrifice to make us truly free! Let's celebrate our Jesus, who didn't just make a proclamation to declare us free but also paid for that freedom with his own blood on the cross.

Thanksgiving: Dead Turkeys Don't Fly

THEME: Thanksgiving is more than a holiday. It should be a way of life.

 === **THINGS YOU'LL NEED** ===

- ☐ *Small Cornish hens (2).* You'll find them at the grocery store, generally frozen. Buy the smallest ones you can find. They're usually under $5, so buy two. One to practice with, and the other for when you're with the kids. A Cornish hen looks just like a turkey but is much smaller . . . so it works great.

- ☐ *Three-person slingshot.* Buy this online. Search under "three-person slingshot" or "water balloon slingshot." They are generally under $35—and often they'll provide a video link so you can see the slingshot in action. The one I bought is called The Beast by Tater Toys. It's described as "Beast 300-yard mega-slingshot water balloon launcher." It works great.

- ☐ *Three people to launch the hen.* The slingshot requires some strength, so you may need some extra adult help on this unless your kids are teenagers. Another family member? A neighbor? Someone from church? Tell them you want them to help launch a Cornish hen—and you'll have no problem finding volunteers.
- ☐ *Wide-open field or park*, someplace to use the slingshot where there's no risk of damaging property or hitting someone with the flying fowl. Are you near a lake? Often launching the bird out over the water is a great, safe option.
- ☐ *Safety glasses*, a pair for each person present at the launch
- ☐ *Hand sanitizer.* If you're handling raw poultry, you'll want to clean your hands well afterward.

Advance Prep

Allow enough time to get the water balloon slingshot sent to you.

You'll want to test this in advance, not just so that you're a bit smoother when you're doing this with the kids but also because you'll need to have a realistic range for your flying poultry. By knowing how far it might fly, you'll be that much safer when you're doing this with the kids. When I did this, the Cornish hen flew 186 feet . . . and I know I could have gotten it a bit farther if I had pulled the slingshot back more.

KEEP IT SAFE

Let the bird thaw entirely before doing this activity. It will be too much like a cannonball otherwise—which would do unnecessary damage.

Running the Activity

Bring the kids and your volunteer helpers (if needed) to your launch site. Again, make sure the bird is completely thawed before attempting this—and that all are wearing safety glasses. If a piece of the slingshot's rubber tubing snapped, you wouldn't want it hitting anyone in the eyes.

Everybody knows that dead turkeys don't fly, right? Well today, we're going to prove them wrong. This turkey—or Cornish hen—just needs a little help to get started . . . and that's exactly what we're going to do. We're going to send that bird up into the heavens!

1. Get your three people in the triangle position to launch the bird.
2. Load the bird into the "ammo pocket" of the slingshot. For greater ease, you can leave the bird in its packaging—although it will look more impressive to see that raw Cornish hen flying through the air.
3. Have one of the kids start taking a video of this special event with a phone.
4. Have one volunteer pull the pocket back, while the other two hold the outside ends securely. I found that by having the two volunteers stand a bit closer together, I was able to pull that Cornish hen back farther—which meant a higher, longer flight.
5. Make double-sure nobody is anywhere near your anticipated turkey crash zone. No joggers or bikers. No swimmers or boats if you're doing this at a lake.
6. Maybe have the kids give a countdown . . . and let that bird fly!

Do the kids want to retrieve the hen and do it again? That's perfect . . . and exactly what you want. But don't send it up again until after you've taught the lesson. Tell them you'd like to talk about something first, and when you're done, they can help that bird fly again.

Remember to have anyone who has handled the raw bird use hand sanitizer.

Teaching the Lesson

Wasn't seeing that bird have one last flight fun? This Cornish hen reminds me of our traditional Thanksgiving turkey. The bird doesn't stay around long. One minute it's getting pulled out of the oven, and the next it's gone. Many times, we won't see a turkey again until next Thanksgiving.

And that's the way it can be with giving thanks. Sometimes we make a big production out of giving thanks—but it doesn't last long. Some families go around the table so each person can say what they're thankful for. There is a lot of emphasis on giving God thanks on that one day . . . but often that's it. Like that bird in the slingshot, we launch our thanks up to heaven and then it's over. We're done.

Just like dead turkeys really don't fly, sending our thanks up to God once a year doesn't really fly with him, either. Would you agree with that?

> Rejoice always, pray continually, give thanks in all circumstances; for this is God's will for you in Christ Jesus. (1 Thess. 5:16–18)

What if we don't feel we have anything to be thankful about?

Does this Scripture passage say we have to be thankful about the hard times—or are we instructed to develop a thankful heart, to find things to be thankful about even when we are having hard times?

How can we give thanks in all circumstances? What can we possibly have to be thankful about when we're going through a hard time?

- We can be thankful that we aren't alone. **God promises never to leave or forsake us.**
- We can be thankful that **God has saved us, loves us, and wants to hear from us.**
- We can be thankful that **God gives us his Holy Spirit** to comfort us, teach us, and grow us to be more like Jesus.
- We can be thankful that **God has a purpose for us**—and that he promises to use even the hard things for our good.

If we get in the practice of finding things to be thankful about—even when we're going through hard times—how might that benefit us and those around us?

If we are more grateful, that will also guard us from pride, bitterness, anger, envy, and so much more. And we'll definitely be more enjoyable to be around, right?

Summing It Up

When it comes to giving thanks, let's not be like a turkey we only see once a year. Let's not launch a big Thanksgiving Day "thank you" and think that's all there is to it.

Sending the bird on one flight wasn't enough. I know all of you would like to see that Cornish hen fly again. How would you like it if I said, "No, we've launched it once already today. We can do it again next year." Wouldn't you be disappointed?

God would feel the same way if we didn't regularly give him thanks. Let's give thanks to God for who he is and what he does . . . and let's do so all year long, okay?

And now . . . let's get that bird and send it flying again!

Road Trip: Lose the GPS, Gain Direction

THEME: It's dangerous to completely rely on others to navigate your Christian life for you. We need to learn to do it ourselves too.

This is likely a devotional you'll be doing while on a road trip or a driving vacation.

THINGS YOU'LL NEED

☐ *Map of the area you're traveling through and to.* An atlas would be nice. You can get either of these online before the trip, or check at the big gas stations—especially those positioned along interstate highways that have a retail store catering to truckers and travelers.

☐ *Highlighter.* To mark your route on the map.

☐ *Nerves of steel* . . . to keep the GPS turned off for an entire road trip day. Yes, that will take some real resolve. Self-control. But do this, and you'll feel some accomplishment at the end of the day that you wouldn't have enjoyed if you'd just let the GPS tell you where to go every mile of the way. And you'll be in a great position to teach the kids an important life lesson!

Advance Prep

First, get familiar with the route you'll be taking. This is what the driver (or designated navigator) used to do to get ready for a road trip before GPS was commonly used.

1. Note where you'll be starting the day.
2. Note where you want to go or where you plan to end up when your drive for the day is done.

Second, get familiar with the map features. Hey, if you need to go through an online tutorial, do it.

1. Note the special symbols and markings on the map so you can point them out to the kids—or answer their questions.
2. Get a feel for the scale of the map. Look for the box showing how many miles are represented by one inch.
3. Be sure to understand the little numbers along your route between cities. For example, you'll see *tiny black numbers* between roads intersecting your route. These give the number of miles between these roads. *Tiny red numbers* generally give cumulative miles between tiny red arrows. Often, you'll see them from one city on your route to the next. By knowing the

exact distance between points on your route, it will be a lot easier to plan out your travel day and have a feel for how long it will take.

4. Take a look at the margins. Maps generally use every inch of space to convey information. Mileage between major cities within the state. State population. How many square miles the state has. Highest point. Tourism phone numbers. Toll information.

5. Take a look at some of the names of towns you'll be passing. Many of them won't be noted on road signs, and some of them are just crazy.

6. Also take note of any parks, mountain ranges, or rivers you'll pass or cross. This just adds some interest to the drive.

Running the Activity

Before you leave, explain to the kids that you're going to drive one complete day of the trip without using GPS. Most kids have only experienced navigation through GPS. Explain you want them to learn to navigate without relying on a phone to lead the way too.

Likely you'll have more than one of the kids take a turn at navigating, so all of them need to understand how a map works. This is your chance to share some of the map features.

- Scale: miles to the inch.
- Red numbers and arrows and black numbers along the route, and what they mean.

Tell them where you'll be starting the drive and where you hope to end.

1. Have them locate and circle the start and end points on the map.
2. Have them highlight the route they'll take all the way to the end point.
3. Have them figure how many miles you'll be traveling (look at the red numbers between arrows for a more accurate number, or use a ruler to get a rough idea).
4. Have them figure about how much time that should take, besides any time needed for gas, bathroom, and food breaks.

Now, throughout the drive, have the kids take turns with the map. They are the navigator. They are the GPS. You'll want to ask them questions during the drive and explain they'll need to know the answer—or be able to figure it out.

How many miles to the next big town?

Where are we approximately on the map right now?

Obviously, they'll want to watch road signs themselves, which can be a huge tool to help them know where you are on the map. When they're navigating, they need to pay attention to the road. It would not be a good time for them to be on their own phone or another screen in any way. Like the driver, they've got a job to do.

If you'll be stopping at a hotel, you may have to phone their desk to get directions from the road you'll be on. No cheating by using the GPS—even though it would be soooo easy.

Teaching the Lesson

The teaching will likely come later, maybe still as you're driving—but I'd wait until each of the kids who will be navigating has had a turn.

What have you learned that you didn't know before?

What kinds of information does the map have that you didn't realize it had?

Did any of you feel a sense of accomplishment that you figured out where you were and where you needed to go without the help of technology and satellites?

Did it feel good not having to rely on someone telling you where to go every mile of the way?

There are some real parallels to the Christian life. Sometimes we can fall into the habit of using a different kind of GPS: the Guiding Pastor System. We rely on the pastor to tell us where we are, where we need to go, and what to expect along the way. If we don't have the pastor, we'll likely get lost. A pastor is important, to be sure. But we also need to learn to navigate life ourselves.

This is a really obvious question, but what "roadmap" has God provided for us to navigate through life?

> Your word is a lamp for my feet,
> a light on my path. (Ps. 119:105)

The Bible is like a map, showing us the way. And we need to learn how to use it accurately.

> Do your best to present yourself to God as one approved, a worker who does not need to be ashamed and who correctly handles the word of truth. (2 Tim. 2:15)

As we learn to study the Bible, we'll see how God uses it to lead and guide us to the right destinations in life. We'll also see how it can keep us from steering to bad or wrong places. Places that will hurt, damage, or trap us.

The highway of the upright avoids evil;
>   those who guard their ways preserve their lives.
>   (Prov. 16:17)

Summing It Up

Learning to use a map is a good skill to have, especially if you lose your phone and have to find your way someplace. And learning to read and use the Bible as a map is so much more important than that.

We won't always have a pastor at our side to help us with a question, a problem, or direction for where to go. But if we learn to find the answers ourselves, we'll be able to keep going. We won't end up lost. If we use this map God gave us, life will be kind of like a great road trip. We'll end up going to some pretty amazing places.

And like we paid attention to all those little details on the map to help us know where we were and how to get where we were going, don't forget to use the entire Bible, both Old and New Testaments. We'll find essential help and information and encouragement by using the whole thing.

> All Scripture is God-breathed and is useful for teaching, rebuking, correcting and training in righteousness, so that the servant of God may be thoroughly equipped for every good work. (2 Tim. 3:16–17)

Ocean Shore: Tide Chart

THEME: Tide charts are wonderfully reliable, and people depend on them for their jobs and safety. As Christians, we want to have a reputation for being reliable and dependable too.

This is likely a devotional you'll do when you're by the ocean, but that doesn't have to be the case.

THINGS YOU'LL NEED

☐ *Tide chart.* You can pull this up online for whatever area of the coastline you're visiting.

Advance Prep

Have the tide chart all set so you don't have to look it up while the kids are waiting for you to start, especially if you're doing this while you're on vacation.

And if you are on vacation, the best place to do this may be at the shore or the docks. The kids can observe the high tide marks that way, and the whole importance of the tides will make more sense.

Familiarize yourself with the chart just a bit. The two things you'll want to refer to are how exact the times are of the high and low tides, which are dependable right down to the minute, and how many feet of difference there are between high and low tide.

Running the Activity

Show the kids the tide chart, emphasizing how it gives the exact time for high and low tides.

You could look at this chart and know when the tide will be at its highest and lowest today, tomorrow, and a week from now. The tides are dependable, right?

How much of a difference does there tend to be between high and low tide? How many feet does the tide rise and lower?

Where does the water come up on the beach when the tide is at its highest and lowest points? At certain times of the day, you could be swimming—or walking on the sand—depending on where the tide is at the moment.

Teaching the Lesson

Why is it important for the tide charts to be reliable?

Do fishers and boaters depend on that information to get safely in and out of the harbor—possibly to keep from hitting rocks, reefs, or sandbars when the tide is low?

In a way, we as Christians can be like a good tide chart—or not. We can be dependable. Reliable. What might that look like, if we were really reliable and dependable as a person in general?

- If we say we'll do something, we'll do it—and right on time.
- If we say we'll be someplace next week at a certain time, we'll be there.
- If we agree to work on a project as part of a team, we'll do our part to the best of our ability, without reminders and without complaining.
- If we say we'll get some job or homework done, we'll make sure it happens—without needing to be reminded.

What might it look like if we were just as reliable and dependable as a Christian?

- We'd be working on being more like Jesus, conforming to his Word.
- When we messed up, we'd be quick to apologize and strive to make it right.
- We'd pray about the things we do, asking God to lead us and not just doing what we feel like doing.

We could add a lot to this list. But what we're talking about here is our reputation. A tide chart is known for being accurate. It is dependable. We can rely on it. Fishers and boaters risk their lives on the accuracy of those charts. And as Christians, we want to develop a reputation for being reliable and dependable too. That means we work at doing the right thing

- even when it's hard.
- even when we're tired.
- even when nobody else is doing the right thing.
- even when we're scared.
- even when we'd like to quit.

> A good name is more desirable than great riches;
>   to be esteemed is better than silver or gold. (Prov. 22:1)

We all develop a reputation . . . good or bad. The Bible reminds us that a good reputation is extremely valuable. If we have a reputation for being reliable and dependable—as a person in general and as a Christian—how might that impact our relationships with friends and family?

Summing It Up

If tide charts stopped being dependable and reliable, boats would be wrecked, businesses would be lost, and some people might even die.

And if we aren't dependable as a person and as a Christian, how might others be negatively impacted?

Let's develop a reputation for being reliable and dependable. We can definitely ask God to help us do that.

The Beach: Washout

True Christians can't stop at just knowing the Word. They need to put it into practice too.

This is likely a devotional you'll do when you're by the ocean or a lake with a beach.

THINGS YOU'LL NEED

- ☐ *A beach.* We're doing this devotional as if you're vacationing at the beach. If that isn't the case, you can do this somewhere with a big sandbox.
- ☐ *Large bucket filled with water.* If you can have two or more buckets of water available, that's even better.

Advance Prep

No advance prep needed on this one. Hey, you're on vacation!

Running the Activity

Take the kids to the beach and have them build a sandcastle in the wet sand. Go as big and elaborate as you like—but keep an eye on the clock. You don't want them to tire of the activity before you teach the lesson. Give the kids a hand so this is a family project. When you think the castle or fort is beginning to look impressive, move on to the lesson.

Teaching the Lesson

Remember the story Jesus told about the wise and foolish builders? He said,

> Therefore everyone who hears these words of mine and puts them into practice is like a wise man who built his house on the rock. The rain came down, the streams rose, and the winds blew and beat against that house; yet it did not fall, because it had its foundation on the rock. But everyone who hears these words of mine and does not put them into practice is like a foolish man who built his house on sand. The rain came down, the streams rose, and the winds blew and beat against that house, and it fell with a great crash. (Matt. 7:24–27)

This passage talks about and compares two kinds of people. And it pretty well describes the two kinds of people we find in churches today.

What is one thing they have in common? They both hear the Word. But what they *do* with the Word they hear is very different.

What does Jesus point out? One puts the Word into practice—and the other doesn't.

What does it mean to put the Word into practice?

- We put the Word into practice when we actually obey what the Bible says.
- We put the Word into practice when we consistently apply what we're learning in the Bible to our own lives.

Does putting the Word into practice mean we never mess up? No, but we aren't sloppy with obeying either. If we are putting the Word into practice, our regular habit—or *practice*—should be to obey God and the principles in his Word.

How does Jesus describe the end result of the two builders . . . the consequences of the choice each one made?

- The one who chose to put the Word into practice survived the storm.
- The one who chose to ignore the Word and not put it into practice lost everything in the storm.

The passage is using a word picture to describe how smart and wise it is to put the Word into practice. It's as if Jesus is saying something like, "Do you know how wise it is to put my Word into practice? It's like a person who secures the foundation of their home to solid rock, knowing a storm is coming. That's how wise that person is."

And Jesus goes on to give us a word picture of just how bad and foolish it is to hear what the Word of God says—but ignore it and fail to dedicate ourselves to obeying consistently. It's as if Jesus is saying something like, "Do you have any idea how foolish it is to hear the truth of my Word and fail to put that into practice in your everyday life? It's as foolish as someone who builds their house on sand—right on a beach—with a Category 5 storm rolling in."

I want to help you remember this really, really important truth about the Christian life. And I have a bucket here. Let's attack this sandcastle like we're a really bad storm.

If you can get the kids to join in with swamping the castle, that would be great. The more they are involved, the longer they will remember the lesson. You may need to go back to the ocean several times to refill the bucket(s). The objective here is to fully demolish it.

Summing It Up

Well, it looks like our sandcastle has been destroyed. And that's what happens to the lives of all those who hear what the Bible says but don't put it into practice. It may not happen as quickly as we took out the sandcastle. In fact, often those who aren't careful to put the Word into practice may appear as though life is treating them really well. But remember, Jesus doesn't lie. He makes it clear that people who choose to ignore his Word will eventually face great, horrible loss.

I want you to be among those wise ones who do what Jesus says. So let's each pick one thing from the Bible that we want to put into practice, starting today—with God's help.

I'll list some questions to get us started, in case your mind is a blank. Ask God to show you where to begin.

Read the entire list, part of the list, or add your own things to the list. Just do what you need to do for your family.

Do I need to forgive someone?

Do I need to be less selfish and start thinking of others first?

Do I need to stop arguing?

Do I react well when I have strong emotions, like anger?

Do I need to stop complaining so much?

Do I need to confess when I've been dishonest—and work at being truthful?

Do I need to speak with kindness more consistently?

Do I need to be kind to someone in particular whom I've not been kind to?

Do I spend time in the Word regularly?

Do I actually think about the words I'm singing in church . . . and mean them?

Do I need to protect someone who is weaker than I am?

Do I honor God as Lord of my life?

Do I honor Mom and Dad consistently?

Do I need to change my language when I'm with others?

Do I need to stop being so proud and truly be more grateful for the abilities and opportunities God has given me?

It's critical that we are wise and put the Word into practice. Here's what I'm going to work on—and ask God to help me with. *As a parent, you'll want to share what you should work on. Otherwise, you're sending a "do as I say, not as I do" type of message.*

And I'd like to know what each of you chose to work on too, so we can help and encourage each other to put the Word into practice.

As we put the Word into practice, realize we are doing something really good for our lives now. But this is also something that's critically important for our future—because hard times and storms will come into our lives. By building our strong foundation now, we'll be ready when those storms come.

Trail Hike: Trailblazing

THEME: The Bible gives us paths to stay on—and if we leave them, we put ourselves at risk.

This is likely a devotional you'll do somewhere out in the country, somewhere you'll find hiking trails.

THINGS YOU'LL NEED

- ☐ *Access to a trail* for a family hike
- ☐ *Compass* or a map app on your phone
- ☐ *Other gear for a safe hike.* Water. Food. First-aid essentials. Pocket-knife. Flashlight. Backpack. Bug spray. Sunscreen. Maybe even an appropriate weapon, depending on where your trail is located.

Advance Prep

If a trail hike isn't something your kids would enjoy, consider skipping this devotional or saving it for another time. You want them to *want* to do this. If they go into this complaining, you'll have a hard time pulling off a meaningful devotion.

1. Choose a trail that is a good fit for your family. It would be great if you've actually hiked the trail yourself, beforehand, but if you're doing this on a family vacation, that would be hard to do.

2. If you aren't familiar with the trail, get some good, reliable, local information. I've been on some trails that seemed a lot longer than what was marked on the map. And I've been on some trails that were really, really poorly marked.

3. Be sure you know what terrain and wildlife you'll be facing, and if that's something you want to do as a family. If you're in an area where there are poisonous snakes or dangerous animals, think twice about taking the trail. Find another one. And if you do choose to take a trail where there is a risk of dangerous creatures, be sure to keep the kids close . . . not running off ahead.

Running the Activity

Have the kids help you pack for the hike. Especially when it comes to the snacks—and the weapons. If they want candy bars instead of granola bars, I'd go with the candy. If they believe each of you should carry a pocketknife, well, hey, why not? That already gives them the subtle sense that a hike can be dangerous, which will tie in really well to the devotional point you'll make.

Be sure to go over the safety guidelines with them—and the potential dangers. I know some parents won't want to scare their kids.

I'm not suggesting you scare them, but tell them the truth. There are dangers where you'll be going. Again, this sets them up well for the point of the devotional.

Take the kids on the hike. Point out the trail markers or anything else they need to know about staying safe in the area they're in. Let them enjoy God's creation. Will you be crossing a creek? Allow them to get wet. You want this to be a good experience for them. And in this world of entertainment and screens and theme parks, it is a really good thing for kids to find they can totally enjoy the simple things of life.

Especially if you're in an area where there could be dangerous wildlife, be aware of your surroundings—and help the kids do the same. Stop now and then to listen with the kids. This will all help set the tone for the devotional.

Teaching the Lesson

Not long into the hike, stop for a snack break—and to teach the lesson. You don't want to wait until the kids are too tired and hot to listen well.

How fun would it be to blaze your own trail? To totally leave the marked path and just find your own way?

In some ways it could be really fun, but there are also some very real dangers. What might they be?

- You could get lost, for sure.
- You could get hurt—maybe twist an ankle, break a bone, get attacked by an animal—but nobody would know where you were. And if you were far off the path, it would be unlikely that someone would happen to be walking by to help.
- Anybody following you could get hurt too.

How do you think walking a marked trail is a lot like life?

- In the Bible, God gives us clearly marked paths to walk.
- He gives us instructions on how to prepare for the trails of life.
- He gives us guidelines about places we should avoid.

Just like some people think it would be fun to leave the path on a trail hike, many people in life choose to leave the paths God has marked out in the Bible. And it can be fun—for a while. But there is real danger there.

The Bible says a lot about the paths we choose to take in life. It describes the good paths . . . walking in the ways God teaches us. It warns of the bad paths . . . walking in ways God has told us to avoid.

> For the LORD gives wisdom;
>   from his mouth come knowledge and understanding.
> He holds success in store for the upright,
>   he is a shield to those whose walk is blameless,
> for he guards the course of the just
>   and protects the way of his faithful ones.
> Then you will understand what is right and just
>   and fair—every good path.
> For wisdom will enter your heart,
>   and knowledge will be pleasant to your soul.
> Discretion will protect you,
>   and understanding will guard you.
> Wisdom will save you from the ways of wicked men,
>   from men whose words are perverse,
> who have left the straight paths
>   to walk in dark ways,
> who delight in doing wrong
>   and rejoice in the perverseness of evil,

> whose paths are crooked
> and who are devious in their ways. (Prov. 2:6–15)

In a place like where we are right now, we understand how dangerous it could be to just leave the marked trails. I want to encourage you to listen and learn and be careful about the paths you choose in life too.

Sometimes we want to leave the path of what we know is good and right. We think we can leave it for just a short time—then hop right back on. It doesn't always work that way. There are dangers we can't see. Sin has a way of sneaking up on us.

Summing It Up

Most trails are designed to give hikers the maximum experience of a geographic area while minimizing the dangers of hiking in the wilds. Trails allow us to experience the beauty of God's creation without unnecessarily endangering our lives.

And God has given us the Bible as a sort of guidebook through life. A spiritual GPS. He's clearly marked out paths for us that lead to good—and warned us about the hard things that come to those who leave the path.

> In the paths of the wicked are snares and pitfalls,
> but those who would preserve their life stay far from them.
> (22:5)

Let's stay on the path God has for us. And let's be sure we are in the Bible enough to recognize the trail markers of God's paths—and how to avoid the paths that aren't his.

Night Sky in the Country: Blinded by the Light

THEME: Remembering how amazing God is—and how much he cares for us—as we see the stars in the night sky should cause us to follow him more and complain less. As we do, we can be stars to guide others to God too.

This is likely a devotional you'll do out in the country at night, far from city lights that would hide the stars.

THINGS YOU'LL NEED

☐ *Night sky*, somewhere away from the bright city lights

☐ *Green laser pointer.* This can add more interest and awe from your kids. Do a search for "green laser pointer" online. Generally, the ones that work well are between $15 and $30—and you'll find it's worth the investment. Stick with a green one because they shine the brightest and will be visible in the night sky, which is just what you want.

☐ *Extra laser batteries.* Laser pointers burn through batteries fast, especially with how much the kids will want to use it.

☐ *Star app.* This isn't absolutely necessary, but it will be really helpful to use right along with that laser. And it will add so much to the night-sky experience. Do an app search for the free Night Sky app—or any similar app you may prefer. When you hold it up to the sky, it will give you the names and outlines of the constellations above you. You'll be able to use your laser pointer to point them out to the kids.

☐ Another nice feature of this app is to pinpoint the International Space Station as it orbits past. A complete orbit of the earth only takes about ninety minutes, so you can plan your outing to be sure you'll see it. Once the app has helped you locate the space station, you can use the laser pointer to help the kids see it.

Advance Prep

Order that green laser well in advance of your trip. You'll want to test it on your own before you leave. It's stunning how far that beam will travel at night! Try lighting up things in the distance, and definitely use the laser to point up into the night sky. You'll be amazed at how easy and fun it will be to point clearly at stars this way.

Install the free Night Sky app before you leave. That will give you a chance to get familiar with it before doing the devotional with the kids. See how it will help you identify constellations and locate the International Space Station.

KEEP IT SAFE

Be sure to follow all the safety rules that come with the laser pointer. A couple quick reminders here:

- Do not allow the kids to point the laser at anyone else. Not at family. Not at cars, trucks, or unsuspecting strangers in the distance.
- Do not allow the kids to point the laser at a mirror.

Generally, when kids understand you'll only let them use the laser if they handle it right, they'll follow the instructions.

Running the Activity

When you're traveling and you're someplace far from city lights, take your kids out to see the night sky. If you live anywhere near a town or city, odds are the kids don't get a chance to see nearly as many stars as they can at your vacation spot.

1. Give them a few moments to take in the immensity of the universe above them in the night sky—at least that part they can see.
2. Let them have turns pointing at various stars with the laser pointer.
3. Pull up the app and identify some planets, constellations, and the International Space Station, using the laser pointer to help point them out.

God definitely did amazing things when he created the stars, didn't he?

Teaching the Lesson

> By the word of the LORD the heavens were made,
> > their starry host by the breath of his mouth. (Ps. 33:6)

Why do you think God created so many stars?

- We know stars were created to give some light at night—so people can see to a certain extent.
- We know stars were created to help us know where we are . . . to help navigate. Stars were used by sailors and fishers for centuries to find their way back home.
- I think stars were also created to give us a sense of awe and wonder and to help us see how big and powerful God really is. The more astronomers learn of the universe, the bigger they find it to be, filled with more stars than any human can count. The fact that God knows how many stars there are—and has named each one—shows how incredibly amazing God is. That should cause us to worship God even more than we do.

> He determines the number of the stars
> > and calls them each by name. (147:4)

As we look at the stars, let me read another verse to you.

> When I consider your heavens,
> > the work of your fingers,
> the moon and the stars,
> > which you have set in place,
> what is mankind that you are mindful of them,
> > human beings that you care for them? (8:3–4)

Anybody want to take a stab at what King David was trying to say when he wrote this?

- When we look at the night sky, we see how big and powerful and mighty our God really is.
- And as we grasp that, we should be totally amazed that our God still cares for each of us, who are such tiny specks in the universe. That's something we need to remember; it makes us more humble and more grateful, and it should boost our trust in God and our obedience to him.

As we let the truth soak in of just how much he cares for us, we'll begin to realize how fortunate we are. We should be that much more dedicated to following our God, who loves us and cares for us so deeply. As we realize how blessed we are, we'll be less likely to complain about so many things in life that we tend to gripe about. And as we become more dedicated to following God, if we have that grateful attitude, in a very real way we will shine like stars in a dark night sky. We'll be examples to others. Our lives might be guiding stars to help others navigate to Christ themselves.

Do everything without grumbling or arguing, so that you may become blameless and pure, "children of God without fault in a warped and crooked generation." Then you will shine among them like stars in the sky as you hold firmly to the word of life. (Phil. 2:14–16)

Summing It Up

The stars are out every night. So every night God gives us a reminder of how much he cares for us. That's something to be grateful for, don't you think?

- Let's remember to thank God daily for how much he cares for us.
- Let's remember that because he cares like he does, we have no reason to complain.

May we be grateful for how he cares for us and obey him so that we can be stars to guide others to God as well!

Farmlands: Future Harvest

THEME: We may not see our lives as being worth much more than dirt, but in God's hands he can grow us so that we're a help to countless others.

This is likely a devotional you'd do when passing through farmlands.

THINGS YOU'LL NEED

- ☐ *Packets of seeds*, at least one for each of the kids. Pick up the types of things you'd see growing on farms more than in gardens: *food*, not flowers. Corn. Soybeans. Get as much variety as you can, and ideally choose things that are grown on the farms of the area you'll be seeing.

Advance Prep

You're doing this one likely because you're visiting or driving through areas where your family will be seeing lots of farms.

Now, besides getting the seeds mentioned above, anything else you can do to make this more of an experience for the kids would be smart. Can you arrange for a little tour of a farm? Do some praying and then a little checking on this. Search for a farm market too. Someplace where you can actually see the fresh produce grown locally. You might be surprised at the opportunities you'll find. If your kids get a tiny tour of a farm—or even a chance to see tractors or other equipment right up close—the devotional will be better and will pack so much more power.

Running the Activity

If you're taking them on some kind of tour, perfect. If not, at least drive by some farms. Slow down or find a safe place to pull over so they can see the tractors or other equipment.

Give each of the kids a packet of seeds.

Teaching the Lesson

God has designed seeds to grow into food that can feed people. Now I know this is probably a pretty basic question, but what do seeds need to grow?

- good soil
- water
- sun
- time

Good farmers know exactly what they're doing. They have a plan for the seeds they plant. They know what they want to grow. They plant the right seeds knowing that the crop they'll produce in the end will do real good in the world—and will feed lots of people.

Like a farmer, God has a plan for us—including some good things he wants to come out of our lives. Check out this verse.

> For we are God's handiwork, created in Christ Jesus to do good works, which God prepared in advance for us to do. (Eph. 2:10)

This says God has specific things he wants each of us to do. His plans for me are different from his plans for you—or your brother or sister.

Like farmers make a plan for their fields, preparing the soil and planting seed, God has made plans for what he wants to grow in each of us. He prepares the soil of our lives. How does he water us and get us the essential things we need to grow?

> All Scripture is God-breathed and is useful for teaching, rebuking, correcting and training in righteousness, so that the servant of God may be thoroughly equipped for every good work. (2 Tim. 3:16–17)

If we were to look at a farmer's field before any plants were beginning to grow, it might look pretty sad. Acres and acres of dirt. But farmers know what they've planted. They have a plan for what will come in a future harvest.

When we look in a mirror, we may not see anything that looks much more special than a field of dirt. But the Bible says God has plans for each of us. He has everything prepared. He wants to grow us and grow good things in us. Our job, with the help of the Holy Spirit, is to keep getting nourishment from the Bible and do what it says. If we do, God will continue to grow the seeds he's planted in us to do those good things he's planned.

Summing It Up

Just like it's almost impossible to tell what is going to grow in a field before the seeds start sprouting, it is almost impossible to guess the plans God has for us . . . and the seeds he has planted in our lives for a future harvest. We need to trust him and his plan.

When the crop is harvested, it will effectively feed, nourish, and strengthen so many people. Remember, that is likely what God is doing in you. He wants to raise you to be the kind of person who can nourish and strengthen others in a spiritual sense as well.

Mountains/Hills: Where Does My Help Come From?

THEME: A look at the mountains or hills reminds us of the powerful God we serve—and that he's promised never to leave or forsake us. He's there for us when we need him most.

This is likely a devotional you'd do when traveling through or to a mountainous region.

THINGS YOU'LL NEED

- ☐ *Mountains or hills.* And if the road you're driving on includes tunnels through the mountains, even better.
- ☐ *Phone or camera*

Advance Prep

If you're on a trip that will route you through mountains or hills, think about a place where you might safely pull off the road so the kids can look at the mountains while you teach a tiny nugget of truth. A place where they can do a little climbing in the foothills is even better.

A little background info on the mountains or hills you're in would be helpful. Check that out before you travel there. Maybe you can find an interesting story about the range, or something that happened there in history. At the very least find out the elevation so you can relay some facts to the kids.

Running the Activity

The only real activity to this devotional is when you'll be driving through the mountains or gazing up at them after you park. So this one is low on the "activity scale," but it's also a quick one you can do while traveling.

You'll want all phones or screen devices put away as you're driving through the mountains—at least for the time just before you do the devotional. You want the kids to take in the scenery. And if you're about to go through a tunnel, make sure all the kids are looking out the windows.

Teaching the Lesson

Share any informational tidbits about the mountains or history in that area, then quickly move on.

How are mountains different from sand dunes? Mountains are massive. Amazing. And unlike sand dunes, they aren't going anywhere anytime soon. The wind won't cause them to shift shape or position. Maybe that's why the Bible uses mountains to teach a truth about God.

> I lift up my eyes to the mountains—
>   where does my help come from?
> My help comes from the LORD,
>   the Maker of heaven and earth.
> He will not let your foot slip—
>   he who watches over you will not slumber. (Ps. 121:1–3)

These verses encourage us to look at the mountains and remember where our help comes from in life. Our help comes from the one who made heaven, earth, and the massive mountains in front of us.

Do you think a God who made such big, strong mountains is capable of protecting and helping us?

Do you think a God who made such an immovable object like a mountain is easily moved by changing winds or any difficult situation we might find ourselves in?

This psalm reminds us that he watches over us. How does that amazing thought bring you comfort?

One of the things we think about when we see a mountain is how easy it could be to slip and fall over the side or off a cliff. These verses remind us that God is capable of keeping us from slipping. What types of things might the Bible be referring to when it mentions slipping?

These verses also remind us that God doesn't sleep. Why is that important?

We think of someone who's asleep on the job as one who will miss things. But since God doesn't sleep, he'll never be caught napping . . . never be caught unawares. He is always there.

People tend to hold on to or focus on what they think will really help or save them. What do you see people hold on to?

- **Money.** Many see money as the thing that will keep them from harm.
- **Job.** Many see the right job as the key to making the money that will protect them.
- **Schooling.** So many feel that schooling is the key to a stable life, one where they won't slip off the cliff somehow.
- **Friends or significant other.** Lots and lots of people cling to others, thinking that is the key to security.

This Scripture reminds us that God is the one who can keep us from slipping. From messing up—and getting ourselves hurt in the process. Which suggests he is the one we should be hanging on to, right? How do we do that?

Summing It Up

When we find ourselves in a spot where we're scared, anxious, worried, or overwhelmed somehow, we need a reminder of exactly who it is that we serve. A look to the mountains reminds us of our mighty God and that *he* is our help. The Bible says he won't leave us. He won't let us down. When we're holding tightly to him, he can keep us from slipping.

To him who is able to keep you from stumbling and to present you before his glorious presence without fault and with great joy—to the only God our Savior be glory, majesty, power and authority, through Jesus Christ our Lord, before all ages, now and forevermore! Amen. (Jude 24–25)

That should bring us hope, peace, and joy, don't you think?

A Special Word for Parents

Helping your kids remember the truth of this lesson may require something a little extra. This devo wasn't very flashy, but the truth is rock-solid. It is something your kids need—desperately. And it is the type of thing they may need to remember in the wee hours of the morning . . . when you're asleep and they're awake. Here are two things you'll want to do to help your kids remember this truth.

1. A memento of the life lesson the kids just learned is always a good idea. Can each of the kids find a rock they can bring home from this spot? Something they can put on a shelf in their room? Every time they see it, the rock will be a reminder of the important life lesson you taught here. Take a permanent marker and jot down the reference *Psalm 121:1–3* on the rock somewhere.

2. As you wrap this up, take an individual picture of each of the kids with the mountain in the background, or of them standing at the base of the mountain somewhere. After you get home, print the picture for each of them. They can put it on a shelf in their room with the rock they picked up. Write the verses from the psalm on the back of each picture along with a short message, something like this:

   > Dear _____, always remember who your help is . . . the One who made the mountains. He never sleeps, so even now he watches over you. Hold tight to the One who can keep you from slipping, okay? Love, _____

Florida Everglades or Lakes/ Swamps: Below the Surface

THEME: Before we jump into any situation—no matter how fun or harmless it looks—it makes sense to look for hidden dangers and unexpected consequences. We want to check in with God so he can direct our paths.

You'll likely want to do this devotional when you're traveling by a lake, pond, swamp, or even a river.

 ## THINGS YOU'LL NEED

- ☐ *A lake, pond, swamp, or river.* Ideally, you're looking for someplace where the surface of the water is dead calm.
- ☐ *Binoculars.* Optional, but it's nice if you have them or can borrow a pair.
- ☐ *Powerful flashlights,* if doing this at night. One for each of the kids is ideal.

Now, the activity portion of this devotional isn't extremely active. But the fact that you're taking them someplace *is* the activity. You'll want the kids to take in their surroundings, and you'll teach them while still in that setting.

Advance Prep

The majority of your prep is about selecting a good spot to take your family so they can view that body of water. You'll also want to do some investigating beforehand to tailor the devotional to the place, and perhaps do a little research online.

What kind of wildlife is in the water—or in the area immediately surrounding it? Key in on things that are dangerous or that might make the skin crawl when you talk to your kids about them. Snakes. Leeches. Alligators. Snapping turtles.

What kind of other hazards may be present? Currents. Deep water. Debilitatingly cold water. Rocks or logs hidden below the surface. You'll want to remind the kids that if they dove into the water here, they might be in deep trouble—even if they can't see any dangers.

Are you traveling in Florida, Georgia, Louisiana, Alabama, southern Texas, North Carolina, South Carolina—or anywhere alligators are likely to lurk? Alligators would make a great example of hidden dangers. But don't limit yourself to that. For example, deadly water moccasins hide along the banks of countless lakes and rivers across the entire southern half of our United States.

Any body of water can hold some type of danger. Think leeches . . . those nasty bloodsuckers seem to find us if we venture into lakes and rivers all over the country!

Another option for this activity would be to do it at night. The likelihood of the water being calm at night is higher. And more importantly, almost any body of water looks creepier and more ominous at night. Adding to the creep factor may help drive the point home a bit more effectively.

For the purposes of this lesson, I'm going to go with a lake, pond, or swamp you might find anywhere in Florida, Georgia, Louisiana, Alabama, southern Texas, or parts of North or South Carolina. If you select a different place, be sure to make any needed adjustments as to the wildlife and dangers of that specific area as you teach. Use the devotional below as a template and simply add or subtract the dangers/hazards appropriate for where you're located.

KEEP IT SAFE

Whenever you have kids around water—or potentially dangerous wild-life (snakes, alligators) could be in the area—be sure you're taking extra safety precautions. Clear instructions to the kids are a must, along with plenty of adult supervision. If life jackets are appropriate, be sure the kids are wearing them.

Running the Activity

If doing this in the *daylight*, do your best to explore the lake or body of water with the kids. Did you bring binoculars? This would be a great time to let the kids use them. Talk about the specifics of what you found in your research of the area.

Basically, take a few minutes to look for any signs of dangerous wildlife:

- Are there any bubbles breaking the surface?
- Can you see an alligator or snake sunning on the bank?

- How about the snout of a snapping turtle or gator showing in the water?
- Are there any actual posted signs warning of dangerous wildlife?

If doing this at *night*, use extra precaution to avoid alligators or snakes. Keep the kids close—always. Take a few minutes to absorb the nighttime creepiness of the area.

- Do the flashlights pick up the glowing eyes of any gators?
- What kind of wild-animal noises do they notice?
- Note how still and dark the water is.

Teaching the Lesson

The water looks really calm, doesn't it? But in many states in the South, residents warn that you must assume any lake or body of water has at least one alligator lurking in it. What do you think?

Even if you don't see an alligator, how likely is it that there's one hiding here?

Even if you don't see any venomous snakes, how likely is it that they're here?

Even if you don't see any nasty snapping turtles, how likely is it that they're here?

Might calm water help give you a sense that everything is fine and safe—even if it isn't?

Could there be rocks or submerged logs just below the surface that would hurt you or increase your risk of drowning if you dove right into them?

Could there be currents that might pull you under if you swam in the wrong spot?

Could there be blood-sucking leeches just waiting for an innocent victim to wade into the water—so they can latch on and start draining you?

How tempted would you be to jump into the water and go for a swim without checking the place out really carefully first to be sure it's safe?

Often the most dangerous things are hidden to us—at least at first. That's the same way it can be in life. Sometimes the most dangerous things are not so easy to spot. Can you think of any examples?

Did you ever go someplace or do something that you thought would be harmless—but it turned out to be trouble?

Is there something you might do or someplace you might go that looks harmless—but may not be?

Have you ever known people to be that way? Someone can seem friendly and fun, but as you get to know them you find they are controlling or abusive or not a good influence on you at all.

Sometimes there are things that look fun or harmless, but that is just an illusion. There are dangers that are hard for us to see, but God knows all the hidden things—good and bad. There is no danger that he is not aware of. That's why it makes such great sense to rely on him when we're making choices.

> Trust in the LORD with all your heart
>   and lean not on your own understanding;
> in all your ways submit to him,
>   and he will make your paths straight. (Prov. 3:5–6)

When making decisions, we need to be careful not to think, *Oh, this is an easy decision. I don't really need to check with God on this one.* That's like thinking, *Oh, the water is really calm. I'm sure it's safe to swim here.* These verses in Proverbs talk about how we shouldn't simply trust what we see or think. That is what they mean when they caution us not to "lean on our own understanding." Instead, we need to see God as the boss—and we need to do what our boss tells us to do.

As we do as the Bible tells us to do, acknowledge God knows best and ask him to direct us, and follow the directions we feel he gives us—through reading our Bible, or maybe by a sense we get inside, or through advice from parents—God will direct us. He'll make our paths straight and make the right way clear to us. He'll lead us past the traps and dangers.

Summing It Up

When we look at a lake, pond, swamp, or stream, it's probably easy for us to remember that danger is near no matter how calm and inviting the water may look. We tend to be more careful around water. More cautious.

When it comes to living our everyday lives, it can be a little harder to remember that there are dangers all around. Sometimes we don't think about checking in with God before we make choices about where we go, what we do, what we say or text, or who we choose to hang around with. God sees the things we don't see, and like a good shepherd watches over his sheep, he is all about protecting us.

So before we jump ahead, let's be sure we are checking in with God and asking him to guide us. And if we have some doubts about what we're choosing to do, where we're choosing to go, and who we're choosing to be with . . . we need to pay attention to that feeling.

- It may be God warning us to look before we leap.
- It may be God prompting us to look a little closer at the danger that may be below the surface . . . lurking just out of sight.
- It may be God giving us a nudge to redirect the path we're on.

Before we jump into any situation—no matter how fun or harmless it looks—it makes sense to check in with God. We can ask him to help us see any hidden dangers or unexpected consequences. And we can ask God to help us follow him!

A Special Word for Parents

You put in the effort and taught the kids an extremely important nugget of truth today. Great job . . . you're protecting them! One other small thought: if you'd like to reinforce this with a Bible story at the end of this lesson—or maybe later in the week—check out Joshua 9.1–27. In this story, Joshua and the leaders of Israel are faced with a decision. Honestly? It looked like a no-brainer to these people. The right answer seemed obvious.

These leaders made a decision based on what they saw and felt and believed—based on what was obvious. They trusted that the calm surface wasn't hiding any perilous dangers. Joshua—along with all the other leaders—didn't go deeper by inquiring of God and asking him to direct their decision. As a result, they missed the fact that they were being deliberately deceived. They made a huge mistake. You'll want to key in on verse 14.

The Israelites sampled their provisions but did not inquire of the LORD.

This led to a really, really bad choice . . . one Joshua regretted horribly. (You might also read Exod. 23:31–33.) Because Joshua trusted his own gut and instincts instead of going to God, he messed up on a very specific set of instructions God had given them.

There's a line to an old song that goes something like this: "Better look before you leap, still waters run deep." There's some good truth to that, don't you think?

Theme Park: Good Things Come to Those Who Wait

THEME: **THEME:** The payoffs to being patient.

This devotional is designed to be done when you're traveling to a theme park.

THINGS YOU'LL NEED

☐ *Theme park*

Advance Prep

No real advance prep is needed other than lining up a day at the theme park and determining where/when you'll want to tie in the application in the teaching time. Doing it at the park could work, say, over lunch. Know that there may be more distractions at the park—and the kids will be antsy to get going. If you teach the lesson at the park, don't try to get them to sit down and listen too early in the day. Let them enjoy the park for a while before taking a break. However, if you wait until after the day at the park is over to tie it in, the kids may be exhausted and largely unresponsive.

At the park or after the park—you can make either one work. Be smart and get them a treat or snack while you go over the lesson. If you're doing it on the drive home, stop at a fast-food place or get some ice cream. That will revive the kids long enough for you to get through the lesson.

Because of what you'll be doing at the park, you'll want to talk this all out with your spouse ahead of time so you're both working together on this.

Running the Activity

At some point in the day, pick a ride that is popular and that your kids really want to ride. Is there a long line for it? Perfect. You'll want to get the whole family in line—and you might even talk about how great the ride will be.

Stay in line for at least five, ten, or fifteen minutes. The longer the better. At some point you'll need to switch gears, and this will take some real inner strength to pull off! Tell the kids you think the line is taking too long—and you want to leave to do something else.

The closer you are to the "finish line" when you decide to abort, the better. The kids will likely protest. They'll think you're insane. Be sure to have this all worked out with your spouse so they know what the goal is and how they can help. For example, your spouse can urge you to be patient and ask you to reconsider.

Now, at this point, you have a choice. You can stay in line, or you can leave. You'll be able to teach the lesson either way. They may remember the lesson better if you leave the line—but you may get some real attitude from them too, or even ruin your day. It's your call.

Whatever you decide, adapt the teaching time accordingly.

Teaching the Lesson

I'm going to sketch out this next section as if you almost *left the line, but the kids—and your spouse—convinced you to stay.*

How many of you are glad I decided to stay in line for the ride? Tell me all that I would have missed—and the rest of you would have missed—if I'd insisted we leave.

What is the one character quality I needed a little more of when I was thinking of leaving the line? Patience.

What are some examples, maybe some areas of life, where you or your friends might be tempted to push ahead and do something you shouldn't just because you lack the patience to wait it out?

The Bible says a lot about patience. Let me read you a few verses.

> Better a patient person than a warrior,
>   one with self-control than one who takes a city. (Prov. 16:32)

God values a patient person over someone who is a mighty, conquering warrior!

Be joyful in hope, patient in affliction, faithful in prayer. (Rom. 12:12)

God makes it clear that we're to be patient when tough times come.

> Be completely humble and gentle; be patient, bearing with one another in love. (Eph. 4:2)

God also makes it clear that we're to be patient with others.

In 1 Samuel 13 there's a story about King Saul. While the Israelites were at war with the Philistines, God gave Saul some very clear instructions. Before he was to make any kind of move, Saul was to wait for the priest, Samuel, to get to the camp. Saul waited seven days . . . but then he ran out of patience. He decided to move ahead without Samuel, and in the process he made a huge mistake. He disobeyed God. When Samuel got to camp, he confronted Saul.

> "You have done a foolish thing," Samuel said. "You have not kept the command the LORD your God gave you; if you had, he would have established your kingdom over Israel for all time. But now your kingdom will not endure; the LORD has sought out a man after his own heart and appointed him ruler of his people, because you have not kept the LORD's command." (1 Sam. 13:13–14)

We can be pretty quick to judge Saul for being impatient and messing up, but we can get impatient and mess up too.

Are we quick to get angry?
Are we patient even in the hard times, or do we show frustration because we expect things to go better for us—and right now?
Are we patient with others?
Are we patient to wait for God's gifts to us, or do we get impatient and shortcut God's plans? *If age appropriate, this is a good*

opportunity to remind them of things like sex, which God designed for marriage. But we can get impatient and mess it all up.

Summing It Up

If we had left that line, we'd have missed all the fun of that ride. Sometimes waiting for the things we want or need feels like agony. But remember, our God hears us.

> I waited patiently for the LORD;
>   he turned to me and heard my cry. (Ps. 40:1)

Sometimes we need to work on our patience and on trusting that God will be there for us. The good news is that if we are followers of Christ, patience is a fruit of the Spirit and one of the things the Holy Spirit wants to build in each of us.

When we get impatient, usually that means we're going to make a big mistake—just like King Saul did. Let's not allow our impatience to cause us to miss the things God has for us. Let's ask the Holy Spirit to grow some patience in our lives. We'll be so much better off.

And when Mom or Dad—or someone else—encourages you to be patient, I hope you listen—like I listened when I was urged to stay in the line for the ride. Life will actually be better that way!

Theme Park: Life Lesson from a Theme Park Ride

THEME: Making someone else's day a little bit better doesn't take long—but it's something they won't forget.

This devotional is designed to be done when you're traveling to a theme park.

THINGS YOU'LL NEED

☐ *Theme park*
☐ *Timer.* Using the stopwatch app on your phone works great.

Advance Prep

The only advance prep is to determine where and when you'll teach the lesson. You'll be at the theme park all day, most likely.

Teaching the lesson at the theme park—after some rides—could work, perhaps over lunch. Know that there may be more distractions at the park, and the kids will be antsy to get going. Don't try to get them to sit down and listen too early in the day. Let them enjoy the park for a while before taking a break. However, if you wait to tie it in until after the day at the park is done, the kids may be exhausted and largely unresponsive. At the park or after the park—you can make either one work. Be smart and get them a treat or snack while you go over the lesson. If you're teaching the lesson on the drive home, stop at a fast-food place or get some ice cream. That will revive the kids enough to get them through the lesson.

Running the Activity

Have the kids each choose a ride they really, really want to go on. If they all agree on the same ride, great. If not, do your best to make sure that each of them gets the chance to enjoy their favorite ride at some point during the day.

With each of these rides, activate the stopwatch function on your app seconds before the ride starts. Tuck your phone safely away, and pull it out and note the time once the ride ends. Be sure to record the time for each of the rides.

If you are at a major theme park, you can just check online to see how long the rides are. Often you'll get the ride duration number you need, and that might be easier than trying to time the ride yourself.

Teaching the Lesson

Okay, on a scale of 1–10, with 10 being really, really great, how good was the ride you chose today?

Share how long each ride lasted. Did the duration of the ride surprise you? Did the ride seem longer or shorter than what the actual time was?

So (insert ride name) only lasted (insert the time), but it was a really great part of your day, wasn't it? You'll probably remember it for a long, long time.

To see you have fun on that ride and know it will bring a smile to your face every time you think about it is a really nice thing for me too. I was able to do something nice, and it didn't take long.

That makes me think about how we should do nice things for others. And often the things that will mean the most to others—the things that will bring a smile to their face whenever they remember them—don't really take much time on our part. Or much effort.

Can anybody think of some examples of things you might do to make someone else's day brighter?

- Make an adult's life a bit easier by helping them figure out how to do something on their phone or helping them install an app.
- Say something nice to someone, not to flatter them but to encourage them.
- Send someone a text to encourage them.
- Give someone a sincere thank-you to show appreciation for what they did for you—or for the things they regularly do for you.
- Lend someone a hand when you see they could use it.
- Take the time to talk to someone not as well connected as you are in the youth group.

- Take the time to talk to someone older at church. Ask them about their work, or what they used to do before they retired.
- Give somebody a bit of good news when life is tough for them.

There are so many nice things we can do for others.

- Things that would make their day a little bit better.
- Things that don't take much time.

It may not seem like a big deal, but even Jesus talks about the importance of this type of thing in the Bible.

And if anyone gives even a cup of cold water to one of these little ones who is my disciple, truly I tell you, that person will certainly not lose their reward. (Matt. 10:42)

How long does it take to give someone a cup of water? Not long. See the importance of doing even little, quick things to refresh others—especially followers of Jesus? Not only does it make someone's day better, but Jesus promises to reward our act of kindness.

There is a great account in the Gospels of when a crowd gathered to hear Jesus. They needed food—but there were five thousand of them! Where would they find enough food for everyone? You remember the story, right? There was a boy who offered his lunch of five loaves and two fish, and the disciples brought it to Jesus's attention. However, the disciples didn't see how any sizable good could come from the boy's tiny act of kindness.

Here is a boy with five small barley loaves and two small fish, but how far will they go among so many? (John 6:9)

But Jesus took the boy's lunch and multiplied it until it fed the entire crowd. When the boy offered his lunch, do you think he had any idea just how many people he would help?

Summing It Up

The rides we went on today were short . . . but each made our day that much nicer. The Gospels often show Jesus doing quick little acts of kindness for others. Often these involved healing. Or sharing truth with them. And sometimes he encouraged others just by noticing them—seeing them.

And Jesus can use us to make someone's day better too. Usually it's something really quick. Let's work on that . . . starting now.

Let's brainstorm about something we can do as a family or individually, before we go to bed today, to make someone else's day just a little bit better.

Tim Shoemaker is the author of over twenty books and is a popular speaker at conferences and schools around the country. Over thirty years of working with kids and youth has helped him relate to his reading and listening audience in a unique way. He is a regular contributor to Focus on the Family *Clubhouse* and *Clubhouse Jr.* magazines. Tim loves writing contemporary novels for youth filled with mystery, adventure, and suspense, such as award-winning *Easy Target*, *Escape from the Everglades*, and the rest of the High Water series. His contemporary suspense novel *Code of Silence* was named in the "Top Ten Crime Novels for Youth" by Booklist.

Tim has learned firsthand the need to do more than talking at kids—if you want to hold their attention. And he has found how powerfully object lessons and activities work to convey truth in ways kids never forget. Happily married for over forty years, Tim has three grown sons and three daughters-in-law, lives in Rolling Meadows, Illinois, and still loves working with youth.

CONNECT WITH **TIM SHOEMAKER** AT

TimShoemakerSmashedTomatoes.com

 @TimShoemaker1

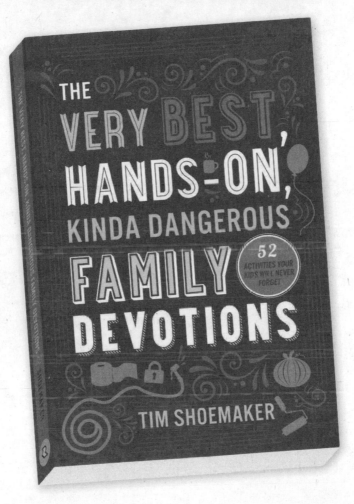